The Countercurrent

ISBN: 979-8-373-531450
Kindle Direct Publishing

for my mothers

4

Prologue

August 1944

The strike of boots on cobblestones and the urgently barked orders stop Hildegard abruptly. She is close to home, but they are closer. She takes a step backwards and flattens herself against the wall. Her heart pounds and she is breathing fast and shallow. She closes her eyes. She is back in a different time, a different place. Her throat tightens and for a moment she cannot move. Even beneath the baking sun, she is cold to the bone. Even here, hundreds of miles away in another city, another country, even now, all this time later, she has not escaped.

She picks out her name in the insistent shouting, mispronounced but clear enough. They have come for her. She knew they would. If they find her, they will send her back. And if they send her back, she opens her eyes, she must not let that happen.

She holds her breath and risks peering around the corner and up the steep narrow street where she lives. There is a group of them outside her apartment building. Four police uniforms, four pairs of polished boots, four unholstered guns. She sees another, larger group march across the top of the street, along the main boulevard. They are everywhere. More shouting from the group outside her building and one of them bangs impatiently on the door with the side of his fist.

She presses back against the wall, squeezes her eyes tight shut and slowly exhales. This is not Berlin, she tells herself, this is not a Nazi fortress, there must be a way to evade them. She must think quickly. Cautiously, she leans around the corner again and looks up. Her eyes scan along the line of the rooftops to the right. The buildings are haphazard, some with flat roofs, some pitched and tiled, some wooden, uneven like a row of broken teeth, punctuated with gaps for the narrow side streets like her own. This maze is familiar to her now, she will find a route through it.

Silently cursing the Romans and the road they built all the way here from Armenia, she slips off her shoes. It is impossible to run on these treacherous cobbles in heels. A final check around the corner, the police are looking the other way, and without another thought she runs barefoot across the road and down the steep stone steps opposite. She enters the labyrinth of alleys that tumble down toward the water's edge.

8

Chapter 1

Neuss, near Dusseldorf, 3 September 1939

With feline assurance, a foot on the chair, the bed, the dresser, then both hands on the windowsill, she propelled herself upwards towards the sky. The air was fresh out on the roof, high above the street and out of the heavy stillness of the apartment. Hildegard filled her lungs and felt the heat gradually disperse from her cheeks. She jammed her feet against the low parapet and slid down to her habitual sitting position, the roof slates warm against her back. Closing her eyes she immersed herself in the peace until her breathing slowed and her mind calmed. She fumbled in her skirt pocket for her packet of cigarettes and lit one, holding the smoke in the back of her throat before exhaling evenly. Her eyes wandered along the tops of the trees beside the canal. Their leaves were fading with the summer, becoming papery yellow ghosts of themselves, spirits clinging defiantly to the branches, reluctant to let go. The trees never failed to comfort her, with their reliably solid form and the satisfying paradox of their constant change. Trees are always never the same, she thought, and knew she could depend on that.

Hildegard thought back to the last time she had retreated up here, almost three months before, following her distressed farewell to Bern at the railway station. "I must go," he had said, with all the tenderness his stiff upper lip would permit, "you know the Foreign Office have ordered us all back. As soon as I have a job and somewhere for us to live, you can follow me. Soon, I promise." He had smiled encouragingly and she had nodded, returning a smile bravely through her tears, trying hard to believe that they would be together again. But there was a quiet whisper of dissent in her head, a whisper telling her that that would not be, that this was the end, and she could not dismiss it.

That day back in June, the roof had given sanctuary, but failed to provide solitude. The whisper had stayed with her and in the weeks since it had grown more persistent. Dear Bern, he was so worried about it all, so determined to get them out of harm's way. Still she could not shake the feeling that it would not come about. Three months on, and despite his best efforts, Bern had only managed to find basic lodgings and no regular work. His last letter, urging her to come to England immediately as the situation in Europe escalated, arrived just yesterday. He sent his love and if anything happens, he wrote, "I wish you the best of luck". What help would luck be, now that war was declared?

A noise inside drew her out of her troubled contemplation and back through the window, blinking as her eyes adjusted to the low light. The attic room was much as it had been throughout her childhood, a few large pieces of dark wood furniture and a bottle green satin eiderdown on the bed. The only addition was the cradle which a brood of cousins and Hildegard herself had occupied in infancy. Now it held her own baby daughter, awake from her nap and smiling. Hildegard picked her up and held her, stroking the back of her head. She closed her eyes and breathed in the sweet, sleepy baby smell as the little girl reached her chubby arms around her mother's neck.

Hildegard's father was calling her downstairs. She hurried from the attic room with baby Eleanor perched on her hip, slowing uncertainly at the top of the stairs when she saw the unmistakable uniforms in the hallway below. She glanced at her parents, Wilhelm, looking indignant at the intrusion and Anna, fretfully twisting the wedding ring on her left hand, and then back at the Gestapos. One of them looked familiar, was he the older brother of a girl she had been at school with? If he remembered her from childhood he did not show it. They were not here on a social visit.

'Frau Reilly?'

'Yes'

'You are under arrest. You will come with us.'

'What?' Hildegard thought she must have misheard him, 'What for?'

'Now hold on a minute,' said her father, stepping forward, 'there must be some mistake.'

The older soldier consulted his papers.

'No. There is no mistake. She is under arrest and will come with us.'

'But, my baby...' Hildegard held Eleanor closer protectively. She felt like she was watching a newsreel in a foreign language, she could see the men talking but could make no sense of what they said. What was happening? Why would they arrest her, she had done nothing wrong? She looked at her parents for reassurance but their expressions reflected her own.

'Leave the child.' The Gestapos were becoming impatient.

Eleanor began to cry at the stern voices and clutched at Hildegard as she handed her to Anna.

'It's alright, sweetheart,' Hildegard did her best to soothe her daughter, but could barely suppress her own rising panic. 'Mummy will be back soon. You be a good girl for Grandma.'

The Gestapos delivered Hildegard to the police station and held her there until the following day. In the morning, she stumbled back blindly through the strangely unfamiliar streets of her home town, wondering how every last reality in her world had changed so completely, overnight. Everything was different now. Without knowing how she had found her way home, she opened the front door and let herself in. Anna was in the kitchen. The relief she felt when she heard Hildegard enter faded in an instant as she looked at her daughter and saw her disheveled clothes, her unbrushed hair, her unwashed, bloodless face.

'Hildegard! What on earth happened to you? We were worried sick when you didn't come home. You are white as a sheet! What happened to you?'

In the safety of the kitchen, Hildegard sank onto a chair and sat with her elbows on the table and her fingers at her temples. The confusion of her arrest the previous day had gone, and the reality of her situation was horrifyingly clear. She leant her folded arms onto the table and lowered her forehead to rest on them.

'Hildegard?'

Anna's anxious questions did not reach her. She did not hear her mother's voice, nor the kettle whistling on the stove, nor the scrape of the chair legs on the floor as Anna sat down opposite her. All she could hear were the metallic echoes and harsh clamour of the police station, the sounds of violence crashing inside her skull. She heard the menace in their taunts. "English whore" they had called her. Dazedly, she lifted her head.

'Where is Eleanor?'

'Asleep, in her pram over there, so I can keep an eye on her. Hildegard...'

'I'm going to have a bath.'

Chapter 2

Berlin, early 1942

'Here we are, Unter den Linden,' said Wilhelm, at last. Unter den swastika more like, thought Hildegard. The trees had been rendered irrelevant, denuded by the season and dwarfed by meticulous rows of towering columns, each claimed by a stone eagle, clutching one of the aggressive black spiders in its claws. A long line of countless red banners with the same hateful emblem whipped in the breeze.

They trundled the last mile along the wide boulevard and turned left just before the river bridge, toward their new home. It had been a tedious journey, the three adults squeezed into the cab of Wilhelm's work truck, with a wriggling three year old Eleanor on Hildegard's lap. Over the last couple of years, the agreeable life they had known in Neuss before the war had slipped away like sand through their fingers, until there was nothing left worth holding on to. At first, Hildegard had tried to escape the unpleasantness by daydreaming of England. On her return from finishing school in Prague, she had secured herself work as an au pair, in Cardiff, which was Wales, not England, she corrected herself. She remembered arriving in the vast art deco railway station filled with light and life and how, as she sat waiting to be collected, she had felt like she belonged there, fitting in like the last piece of a jigsaw, a picture of nineteen thirty-six. That feeling of belonging there had grown and her life then felt open to countless possibilities. The people were all so friendly and she had her independence and a job she enjoyed and her confidence in the language was increasing and the country was beautiful and she, breathlessly, loved it all.

Then, she had met Bern, the most English of Englishmen, as only one who had grown up in the colonies could be. He was twice her age, and she thought him terribly sophisticated and charming, if a little laconic. She did her best to appear sophisticated too, and was grateful that, if nothing else, she had learnt at the finishing school how to smoke a cigarette in company without choking. She had thought that Bern was amused by her youthful sense of wonderment and their relationship took off in a giddy whirlwind. They married the following year when Hildegard had just turned nineteen. Very shortly afterwards they went to live in Cyprus where he was a Government forester.

He had loved her, she was sure of it, and their daughter, and she could not understand his silence since the start of the war. No letters had arrived from England at all. The thought crossed her mind that Bern could have asked their Greek friends in Cyprus to forward a letter for him, at least at the start. Perhaps he had not thought of that. Or what about the Red Cross, they could trace people, couldn't they? He had evidently not thought of that either. Sadly, regretfully, she slowly gave up hope of hearing from Bern, let alone of getting any help from him. The letter that she had received as war broke out turned out to be the last that arrived from him. She had no way of knowing if that was due to the censors' diligence or Bern's lack of it. Either way there was no post from England.

During those first years of the war, Hildegard endured the relentless official scrutiny, doing as she was told, for Eleanor's sake and that of her parents, as well as her own. She came to accept that Bern had abandoned them and she was a lone parent to Eleanor. But Hildegard could not rely on her own parents forever, and she felt responsible for how their lives had become difficult too. Previously friendly neighbours now turned away at the sight of them, visiting upon the parents the cardinal sin of the daughter, her marital allegiance to the enemy.

On top of this, the demands of the insatiable war machine on Wilhelm's business were increasing, and the bombing was getting steadily worse. Wilhelm's engineering company was among the many industries that made the Rhineland area a prime target, a target that was within range of the British bombers. Berlin, though, the impenetrable fortress of the Reich, was further east. It offered both greater safety from the bombing, and welcome anonymity. Gradually the family reached the decision, with little other choice, to enter the lions' den.

Wilhelm stopped the truck outside a substantial building owned by the venerable Humboldt University. They had brought few belongings but still it took some time to take everything up the three grand marble staircases and the final narrow wooden one to the attics, with Hildegard and Wilhelm doing all of the carrying. Anna, holding tightly onto Eleanor's hand, conducted proceedings from the entrance steps.

'Not much of a view', said Wilhelm, peering up at grey clouds through the skylight. He could only stand upright along one wall of either of the two bedrooms they had taken, directly beneath the apex of the roof. The furniture was pushed under the eaves, and consisted of a bed, a dresser and a wooden chair in each room. Until very recently, these were humble storage spaces, but they had been promoted to living accommodation as that commodity in Berlin became more scarce.

'Where is my bed?' Eleanor asked with a frown. They teased her a little about sleeping in the bottom drawer of the dresser, but her eyes widened and she bit her bottom lip, so Hildegard pulled the truckle out from beneath her own bed.

'See, you have a special secret bed to sleep in. We'll hide it during the day and make it appear like magic at bedtime.'

Eleanor leapt onto the cot, delighted. The attics were snug, but they would be adequate for the three of them with Eleanor still being tiny and Anna and Hildegard both petite. Once all of their things were installed, Wilhelm left them to make the long drive back to Neuss and his business.

Life in Berlin quickly found its rhythm. Hildegard's walk to work took a brisk twenty minutes in the morning, but sometimes longer on the way home if she had errands. She enjoyed working again, she had not had a job since she was married more than four years ago, and then Eleanor was born fifteen months after that. Now she taught English at the Berlitz Language School, which resided in an elegant building with tall windows, on the corner of Leipziger Strasse and Wilhelmstrasse. It was true that working to support herself and her family was a necessity, but it also felt like validation. It took strength, but it gave her strength too, and a new sense of purpose that began to dilute the sadness of her lonely circumstance.

Hildegard had her own classroom in the Berlitz School and was addressed therein as Mrs Reilly. She had worked hard on perfecting her English and spoke it fluently, without a trace of an accent. In line with the school policy of total immersion of students in their chosen language Hildegard spoke only English to her students, who made the tacit assumption that she was a native speaker. The students were mostly junior government officials, keen to demonstrate faith in the Fuhrer's plans for expanding the Reich's boundaries to include England, and ready to take up their positions in the new world order when they did. They were diligent and respectful and Hildegard was gratified by their progress and the good rapport she built with them over the first few weeks of teaching.

One morning, a new student arrived. When everyone had taken their seat, Hildegard welcomed him to the class.

'Good morning, my name is Mrs Reilly, I am your teacher. What is your name?'

The young man stared at her. He was the archetypal Aryan, with an athletic build too big for the classroom chairs, blond hair, ice blue eyes, and a cold air of arrogance. He did not speak. Hildegard tried again, she put her hand to her chest,

'My name is Mrs Reilly. You say, "my name is", and then introduce yourself.' She opened her palm to him, to indicate his turn. Again there was no response. She consulted her register for the name added at the bottom of the list.

'It's Reinhardt, isn't it? Try this, "my name is Reinhardt".'

'Ich heisse Reinhardt', he said, mocking her.

'Reinhardt, I'm sure it has been explained to you, in this class, we speak only English. Will you try, please, "my name is Reinhardt"?'

The rest of the class were all staring at the newcomer now and shifting uncomfortably in their seats. Hildegard paused, uncertain what to do if he continued to challenge her. Whilst she was confident of the support of the school over an issue of discipline, you could never be sure what connections a person might have, nor what consequences that might bring, however justified your actions. She was, after all, officially an enemy alien.

The young man considered her request, looking haughtily around the room, checking he had his classmates' complete attention. Satisfied, he conceded, repeating the sentence as she had asked. He smiled at her then, humourless and superior, pleased with himself for asserting his authority. Hildegard concealed her relief behind setting a written task that required nobody to speak.

At the end of the lesson, as was her habit, she stood at the door saying goodbye to each student, encouraging their various farewells.

'Goodbye'

'See you next time'

'Good day to you'

The new student was the last to leave.

'Ich heisse Reinhardt. Heil Hitler, Frau Reilly.'

He towered over her, staring down into her face, emphasising the jagged, guttural pronunciation of his mother tongue. Hildegard lifted her chin, calmly meeting his gaze.

'Speak English, please, Reinhardt,' she said. A second later he turned away and with a short laugh strode off down the corridor.

Hildegard took her cigarettes from her bag with a shaking hand and went to open the window.

Chapter 3

Eleanor was playing with her doll on the first flight of the grand staircase in the Humboldt building. Once the doll was dressed to Eleanor's approval and sitting upright on the step next to her, she lost interest and found her attention drawn toward the doorway of the kitchen. She perched her nose on an iron curlicue in the balustrade and peered through the metal swirls, watching the kitchen ladies. It looked nice in there, the radio was playing and the ladies chatted and laughed as they worked. It smelled nice too, steamy scents of cleaning and cooking, like someone's home. Eleanor was allowed to play on the stairs because the ladies had promised Anna they would keep an eye on her and she was a good girl, she would stay where she was told. One of them saw Eleanor watching and called her in to the kitchen.

'Hello there. You are being very good, your Grandma said you would. Come in here with us and we'll see if we can find something nice for you.'

The lady was smiling at her and beckoning her in. Eleanor picked her doll up by the hand and walked slowly down the last few stairs. She stopped in the doorway, wary of venturing further, but more encouragement, and the cup of milk and a plate with a small slice of yellow cake on it on the table persuaded her.

'We don't often make cake, but it's one of the professors' birthdays today so you're in luck!'

'Thank you', said Eleanor. She sat with her doll next to her and ate quietly, careful not to make crumbs on the table.

'You look like a little doll yourself,' said the lady, 'with your big blue eyes and pretty curls.'

Eleanor smiled shyly at the youngest of the kitchen ladies who was speaking to her. She had a bright smile and laughter in her voice and Eleanor liked her for being kind, but she did not know what to do with so much attention.

'Oh! Lale Andersen! My favourite, can we turn it up a little?' The lady turned away from Eleanor and went toward the radio.

'It's already quite loud,' said one of the others, 'we don't want to annoy the professors.'

'Vor der Kaserne
Vor dem grossen Tor' the younger woman sang along.

Eleanor thought the song had a pretty tune, and she listened carefully to the words. It was about a soldier leaving his barracks to go off to the war and having to say goodbye to his sweetheart, who was called Lili Marleen. Eleanor did not know what the soldier's name was, but she thought he must be one of the men at the Zeughaus barracks around the corner, because there was a lamp post outside there, just like in the song. It was quite a sad song, Eleanor thought, but she liked it anyway. It was swirly, like waving a ribbon in the air, not shouty and frightening like some of the other music she heard.

When Hildegard came into the kitchen on her return from work, she found Eleanor carefully sweeping around the chair legs with a dustpan and brush. The ladies made a great deal of how helpful she had been, and said she was welcome to join them again. Eleanor tucked her doll under her arm, taking care to let her face forwards so she could see where they were going, then smiled and waved goodbye before taking Hildegard's hand for the long climb upstairs.

'I'm sorry I'm a little late today,' Hildegard said wearily on the way up, 'I had an errand after class, it took a bit longer than I expected.'

There was only some bread and a meagre slice of cheese each for supper, both the result of some dogged searching that day by Anna. They were all tired anyway and decided on an early night.

A few hours later the dread wail of the air raid siren woke them. Bombing raids were not as frequent in Berlin as they had been in Neuss, and did not last as long, but still they were prepared. Already dressed from going to bed in their clothes, Hildegard slipped on her shoes and with Eleanor under one arm and the little case packed ready by the door under the other, hurried down the many stairs with Anna close behind. Once in the street, they joined the stream of grim-faced people heading to the public shelter nearby.

Eleanor was screaming but there was no time to stop and comfort her, the officious wardens were blowing whistles and ordering everyone to hurry. There was no option but to obey them, they could and would report anyone who failed to observe the air raid regulations. Once inside the shelter, they picked their way across the already crowded floor to some space and sat to wait out the raid. Eleanor stopped screaming immediately she was set down. 'No need to cry, we're safe in here,' said Anna. 'She must have been frightened being woken up like that.'

Hildegard lifted her little daughter into her lap where she curled up in her arms and went back to sleep. It was not fear that had made her scream, but outrage at the humiliation of being carried all the way under her mother's arm, feet first.

Chapter 4

Aside from Reinhardt's habit of delivering after class news bulletins, in German, on the glorious progress of the Wehrmacht, Hildegard enjoyed her job very much. He tried her patience, but aware that that was his intention, she held fast in her reaction to him with a measured daily reminder to speak only English in the classroom. Sometimes she returned home early enough to collect Eleanor from the kitchen on her way in. Often though, Anna had already taken her up to the attic, if Hildegard did not go straight home after class.

As Hildegard settled in to her job, so Anna and Eleanor's days also found a routine. It mostly consisted of queuing with the shopping coupons, and perhaps a walk in the Tiergarten afterwards if they felt up to it. Eleanor had developed a worrying susceptibility to episodes of bronchitis. The little girl would cough and cough, her face pale and dark eyed, her throat too sore and swollen to swallow. She was not eating properly even when she was well, and Hildegard knew that she needed better than the colourless rationed diet to restore her health. She had heard about a place where people were selling homegrown fruit and vegetables and resolved to venture out there to see if she could buy anything.

A few days later on a crisp spring day, Hildegard alighted a train at Charlottenburg station. She was smartly dressed in her brown pinstripe skirt suit, which was a cast off from Wilhelm that Anna's skilled tailoring had transformed to a feminine cut, and a new hat, the only concession to fashion as yet unrationed. She had a firm grip on her little mock crocodile case. It was improbably weighty but she carried it lightly, happily looking forward to getting home in the late afternoon sunshine.

The train was already at the platform when Hildegard arrived and knowing she was unlikely to find a seat, she placed the case at her feet ready to stand in the corridor. Just before the guard closed the door, two young Gestapos got on behind her. She felt her palms begin to sweat.

'Good afternoon, Miss, Heil Hitler.'

'Good afternoon,' Hildegard said, 'Heil Hitler,' the ubiquitous, compulsory greeting.

Hildegard turned to look out of the window, fixing her face in a neutral expression, sure they could hear her heart pounding. The Gestapo's resumed their conversation, but few minutes later, they addressed her again.

'Going away, or returning home?' said the taller one, indicating her case.

'Oh. Going home,' Hildegard smiled politely, glancing at them before turning back to look out of the window. A line of perspiration trickled down her spine.

'Just a short trip away, then? With such a small case?' They persisted and Hildegard was forced to engage with them, she could not risk causing offence.

'Yes, it was. Just a short trip. Oh, this is my stop, excuse me,' she said brightly, as the train slowed to a halt. Her hand closed around the handle of the suitcase just as the Gestapo nearer to her also reached to pick it up.

'Let me help you with that.'

'Oh, no need, I can manage. Thank you!'

Hildegard stood up with the case in her hand and stepped quickly off the train. She walked briskly along the platform and resisted looking back but she was sure she could feel their eyes on her. The platform seemed endless but as Hildegard finally reached the exit the train pulled away, exhaling clouds of steam. She breathed out with it.

'You look exhausted! You're very late, I was worried, what happened? Where have you been?' Anna was waiting at the top of the stairs, twisting the wedding ring on her left hand. Hildegard looked up as the volley of questions fired down fell ineffectually around her, she was only happy to be home. The pitiful sound of Eleanor's cough drew them both inside the attic room, where Hildegard placed the suitcase carefully on the floor and went to comfort her little girl.

'Still coughing, sweetheart?' she said, smoothing the little girl's hair off her face. 'I've brought some things that might help.'

'What happened?' asked Anna again.

Hildegard told them about her trip to Charlottenburg, the train journey home with the two Gestapos, how she had got off the train early to get away from them, and how they had not suspected a thing.

'So, I walked the whole length of Unter den Linden carrying that. My arm feels ready to fall off! But I couldn't let him pick it up, it's far too heavy to have just a few clothes in it.'

Anna picked up the case and immediately set it back down on the floor.

'My goodness, that is heavy. Is it completely full?'

'Open it and see. You'll be cosy tonight, Eleanor, and hopefully it will help your poor cough.'

Eleanor crawled to the end of the bed and peered over to see the case opened. Anna carefully removed the single sheet of newspaper protecting the lining to reveal Hildegard's illicit spoils. They looked at each other, broad conspiratorial smiles on their faces. Black and sparkling and packed in tightly, the case was full of beautiful coal.

'If we're careful, this can last a good few evenings. It will take the chill off at least.'

'Well done, Hildegard. It was risky but this is just what she needs, she's been coughing all day today, poor little thing. She stays warm in the kitchen most of the day, but it is so chilly up here.'

'Oh, I almost forgot,' Hildegard reached inside her jacket and pulled out a small brown paper bag. 'These will help too. They're all for you, I hope I haven't squashed them.'

Eleanor's eyes widened as she looked inside the bag. There lay treasure, perfectly round, perfectly red and scented like heaven. Strawberries! Hildegard had had the great good fortune on her expedition that day to be introduced to a man who had managed to ripen some early under glass and was selling them for an extortionate price. But Eleanor needed them, so Hildegard had bought four at a Reich mark a piece and stowed them carefully for the journey home, they were precious cargo indeed. Anna wanted to mash them to make them easier for Eleanor to swallow and better to soothe her throat, but seeing the little girl's face fall at this suggestion, Hildegard said no, let her eat them whole, "she likes to sink her teeth in."

To her secret relief, her mother and grandmother declined Eleanor's well-mannered offer to share the berries, and she sat cross-legged on the bed, munching slowly, trying to make them last. Hildegard set a fire in the little stove and soon the evening chill was gone.

She had not needed Anna to point out the risks she had taken. The Gestapos had been polite, even friendly, but if they had become suspicious about her, about the contents of the case, if they had asked for her papers, if they had been in a less jovial mood and felt like making a point, finding a victim, there was nothing to restrict their actions, and nothing she could have done to defend herself. When Eleanor was asleep, Hildegard lay in bed thinking about the afternoon. She had managed to get away without any of that happening, the clasps had held, the little case had not spilt its secret, and for that she was grateful. She closed her eyes and watched the perilous journey home replay itself like a film in her head. She watched herself walking quickly along the platform carrying the heavy case as easily as if it held only a few carefully folded items of clothing, silk and lace among layers of tissue. She read her own carefree expression and saw something else there too, a barely perceptible but unmistakable light in her eyes. Today, she had won against the Gestapo. It was a very small triumph, but she was triumphant all the same. The war was now more than three years old and until today, Hildegard had suffered only defeat. She drifted into a deep sleep.

Chapter 5

The news of Erwin Rommel's progress through Africa was relayed faithfully, frequently and with vicarious pride in his great hero by Reinhardt at the end of each lesson. Hildegard would have admired Rommel too, he seemed to be an honourable man, an outstanding professional soldier and a far cry from the Gestapo thugs that she encountered, except that he served the same undeserving masters, and that fact she could not overlook. In any case, she had no intention of either debating Rommel's merits with her student or revealing to him her understanding of his language.

'Rommel hat Tobruk erobert!'
Yes, I know, Rommel has taken Tobruk.
'Speak English, please, Reinhardt.'

'Rommel hat El Alamein erreicht!'
Now he has reached El Alamein.
'Speak English, please, Reinhardt.'

'Rommel kämpft tapfer in Nordafrika. Er wird Montgomery besiegen müssen.'
Bravely fighting. Aren't we all?
'Speak English, please, Reinhardt.'

The news in the last months of 1942 was of fierce fighting on all fronts, and the start, according to Reinhardt, of Rommel's tactical withdrawal in North Africa. Between the broadcast and printed news, and that personally imparted by Reinhardt, Hildegard felt bombarded by propaganda and could make no sense of which side had the upper hand in the war overall, but she knew she could not just sit and wait it out. Berlin felt an increasingly desperate and dangerous place and the threat was mounting as the devastating bombing raids on their home region would inevitably follow them to the capital.

'I think we should move out of the city,' Hildegard said one evening, at the end of a particularly distressing day. She had picked her way to work that morning through clouds of dust and smoke and fresh piles of rubble from the previous night's air raid, trying not to look at the rows of corpses laid out on the road, waiting to be collected, or listen to the inconsolable sobs of the women kneeling next to them. She had heard that this particular building had collapsed after a direct hit and the residents sheltering in the cellar were trapped, but they were not done for by falling masonry or fire, it was the rupture of the hot water main that caused them all to be scalded. There were a myriad ways to die in this war, even for civilians. Her heart went out to the grieving women and she knew she had to find her family somewhere better, somewhere safer to live.
Anna agreed, and within a few weeks they had found a bungalow in a suburb with a railway station that meant Hildegard could travel to work, as long as the line was intact. Eleanor said a sad goodbye to the kitchen ladies, she would miss them. And Lili Marleen, of course. She hoped her soldier came home safely. The new house had a garden though, so the move was not all bad. As far as Hildegard was concerned, it was a

temporary measure until she could come up with a better idea. She was under no illusions that they were completely safe here, but at least the air was fresher which had to be better for Eleanor's cough.

Not long after they moved in, a plane came down in the next street. By some great good fortune, nobody on the ground was injured, and it appeared the pilot had been shot dead before the plane crashed. They clearly were still very much in harm's way, even in this quiet little town. Rumours spread of a secret underground munitions factory and store, which must have been the target for the bomber. If he had hit his mark, they would all have been blown apart.

Hildegard barely noticed the leaves curling and falling that year. Winter arrived entitled, sweeping in and taking over like the once and future king, commandeering the daylight. Christmas made less of an impression, they managed only a muted, pauper's celebration. Even if they had had money for gifts, there was little to be found in the shops, even in Berlin. The town they now lived in could offer just the basic provisions, a butcher, a greengrocer, a baker. Scant meat, few vegetables and almost no flour within made shopping a dispiriting task.

On a cold morning in the new year, Anna and Eleanor decided to try for meat first, and queued patiently at the butcher's, Anna clutching their cards, hopeful of their ration at least. They had not been to this shop before, but the butcher seemed a cheerful fellow, greeting each woman by name, enquiring after their families, apologising for his meagre wares. Inevitably disappointed, his customers left the shop smiling nonetheless.

'Good morning, Mrs.?'

It was Anna's turn. 'Brabender,' she said.

'I haven't seen you before,' said the butcher, his head tilted in question.

'No,' said Anna, 'we've only recently moved here.'

'Ah! Where from?' he was still smiling, all friendliness to the newcomers.

'Berlin,' said Anna, not wanting to divulge more than the minimum of information. You could not assume to trust people you didn't know, when even among friends you had to be careful. The butcher, and everyone in his shop, might be honest, decent folk. Or they might not. They might, for instance, take exception to having a British woman as a neighbour, and make life very difficult indeed for the family. Anna held out their ration coupons to him.

'Of course. What would you like?' he asked, as though he could produce anything they wished for.

'Schinken!' said Eleanor excitedly.

The butcher stared at her. Everybody in the shop stared at her. 'How does a child that age know about schinken?' said the butcher, his genial smile gone and his eyes narrowing with suspicion. Such a cut of meat had not been seen since before Eleanor could possibly remember at her age. Not in a law-abiding butcher's shop like this.

'She has seen a picture in an old magazine,' said Anna, steadily. The butcher nodded slowly. He brought his cleaver down on the block with a thud that made Eleanor jump. They took their ration and left the shop as quickly as they could, Anna in an unspoken pact with the line of women behind them not to acknowledge each other as they passed. Buying on the black market was a widespread practice, but a covert one, whispered of only within a circle of trust. To be suspected of it publicly could be a nail in their coffin in this town of strangers, untested, unknown. They would not return to this shop, Hildegard would have to find that ration in town in future.

That evening, Hildegard came in quiet and exhausted and later than ever from work. Anna indignantly relayed their tale of the butcher's shop to her.

'I wouldn't mind if we had actually had some schinken, but when was the last time we saw that? I hope nobody decides we are black marketeers and informs on us.'

Hildegard was hunched forward a little, forearms on the table, blankly watching one thumb rub the nail of the other. She forced a small, silent nod in response. Anna looked at her daughter's pale, expressionless face. She had retreated inside herself.

'Did you have to go there again?' she asked gently.

Hildegard looked up at her mother with deadened eyes, she watched Anna's lips moving incomprehensibly, then rose from her chair and shuffled slowly to her room.

A short while later, the door opened enough for Eleanor to peer into the gloom. It looked like Mummy was sleeping, and she didn't want to disturb her. She crept in as quietly as she could, and Hildegard felt the warmth of her little body leaning over her, a small hand stroking her hair.

'Good night, Mummy. Grandma says you're not very well, I hope you feel better tomorrow.' Eleanor whispered and kissed the top of her mother's head.

Hildegard did not, could not, move. She heard the door close quietly behind Eleanor, and the tears soaked into her pillow.

Chapter 6

If things had been bad in 1942, in many ways they worsened in 1943. The various challenges of daily life, the rationing, the air raids, Eleanor's bronchitis, travelling around the city, even Reinhardt's insubordination, accumulated and amplified in a horrible orchestration.

Hildegard took every care not to put a foot wrong, but she was wrong inherently, simply for no longer being German. Roosevelt had declared that the war could only end with unconditional German surrender, and since the masters of the Reich showed no signs of faltering in their conviction of supremacy, there was no knowing how long it would last. But despite the impasse, and the apparent hopelessness of her situation, the paralysing fear in which Hildegard had lived since the start of the war was dissipating. She did not debate whether the years of constant threat had numbed her, or whether some previously dormant courage had finally awoken in her, or whether she had simply had enough. The cause was less important to her than the effect, which was that she began to wonder, could she find a way out? A rough sketch of an idea, begun the day after she hit her lowest point, the day after the schinken incident, steadily gained clarity.

Hildegard was frequently delayed in coming home after work, for one or other of a number of reasons. Often, the trains were delayed or cancelled due to damage to the tracks or lack of rolling stock. Even crossing the city on foot was challenging, with frequent new craters and heaps of rubble to negotiate. It was easy to take a wrong turn, when a once familiar street had been rendered unrecognisable by a bombing raid. Sometimes, she was late because she had ventured out to Charlottenburg, where most of the black market food trading was done, to see if she could supplement their rationed diet. But many, many times, she was delayed in Prinz Albrecht Strasse.

The name of the street alone would send a shiver down her spine, synonymous as it was with the building it hosted. The headquarters of the Gestapo was enormous, intentionally built to intimidate anyone with the misfortune of being required to attend. For Hildegard, this was often, and the relentlessly repetitious visits blurred together in her memory. But the first time she had had to report there, soon after they arrived in Berlin, she remembered with merciless clarity.

She had stepped up to the huge main door with trepidation and entered a lobby where a disinterested secretary pointed her down a bleak long corridor, at the end of which were the stairs to the first floor. There were uniforms striding purposefully in every direction, none of them speaking, none of them acknowledging each other, like ants in an ant hill, thought Hildegard. The sharp strike of polished boots on stone floors ricocheted off the walls like bullets.

Another secretary glanced up at her as she knocked and entered the allocated office and ordered her to sit, indicating a wooden bench against the wall. There was an old man already sitting, hunched over on the bench, and Hildegard politely wished him good afternoon as she joined him.

'Don't speak to him. He is a filthy Jew,' snapped the secretary. She got up from her desk and walked around to a filing cabinet, directing a sharp, spiteful kick at the man's ankle as she passed. Hildegard winced and berated herself for lacking the courage to protest on his behalf. The man remained with his head bowed, staring at his hands, one of which was bleeding. He wore a dirty shirt buttoned to the collar but no tie, and crumpled trousers, the ragged remnants of a good suit and his dignity. Hildegard waited until the secretary was not looking, then took her clean handkerchief from her handbag and passed it to him.

'For your hand,' she whispered.

'Thank you,' he turned toward her and she saw his face was bruised and swollen. He was younger than she had initially thought. A tear seeped from the corner of his eye, and Hildegard wondered what else had happened to him that such a small act of kindness would touch him so.

A shrill telephone rang, and the secretary issued another order to Hildegard to go through a door at the far end of the office. Now she entered another office, similar in size to the first but far more opulent. There was a rich carpet on the floor, oversized oil paintings on two walls and a deep buttoned leather sofa. From behind the vast desk, a Gestapo watched her close the door and walk a few steps into the room.

Afterwards, she could not recall how long their interview lasted, his stock questions were entirely predictable from the numerous such interviews she had endured in Neuss. Where did she live? Where did she work? Who did she see? Where was her husband? Answer the questions, Hildegard, and then you can go home, she told herself. More questions. Stay calm, be patient. Always the same questions, over and over again. From time to time he would stop speaking and stare at her, the inescapable, paralysing gaze of a predator on its cornered prey. Hildegard felt the panic of that trapped animal rising inside her.

Eventually he closed the manilla file on the desk and pushed back his chair. He stood and walked over to the door, and Hildegard, with some relief, stood too.

'Oh. I thought we had finished,' she said. He had locked the door.

'Not quite.'

He turned back toward her. The blood drained from her face and her hand reached for the back of the chair to steady herself as she saw he was unbuckling his belt.

There were more repetitions of this episode over the next year and a half than Hildegard cared to count. She chose not to recall their names or faces, their voices, their sweat and sour breath, the unwelcome weight of them, anything that made them human. In her mind, they were featureless, odourless, blank and silent as artists' mannequins, stripped of the human textures and shades from which memories form. They were the homogenous embodiment of callous violence. They were Gestapo, a uniform, a cruel and repellent concept, not a person. What they did was an act of war, of domination and humiliation which they did because they could, because they thought they were gods and beyond retribution. For years, since the very beginning of the war, the day of her first arrest, she had feared Gestapo. The fear was always with her like an invasive parasite, capable of overwhelming all other emotion. The fear could control her.

Chapter 7

The seasons of 1943 were each marked by a significant event for Hildegard. The first was a consequence of her visits to Prinz Albrecht Strasse, when the trees were bare and heaps of dirty snow littered the ground. Several times before, she had had cause to seek out a mean and judgmental woman in a seedy flat above a tobacconists in a narrow forgotten street just off the city centre. The tobacconist himself had become adept at determining at a glance which anxious young women entering his shop he should direct to the rickety back stairs, which he did without comment, just a slight incline of his head. Another poor fool to see the angelmaker. This time was Hildegard's fourth and final abortion. It was by far the worst.

'You've left it late this time,' the woman said, thin lipped and emotionless, as if Hildegard were there to post a parcel. She took her needles from a drawer in the dresser. 'It'll be more difficult.'

Afterwards, Hildegard wrapped her coat tightly around her, drawing her shoulders in, holding herself together, and head bowed, trudged back through the filthy snow to the station. She concentrated only on putting one foot in front of the other, and the thin trail of red black blood seeping down to her instep went unnoticed. She had no recollection of her journey home. It was the day of Anna and Eleanor's schinken incident at the butcher's, a few weeks after they had moved.

In the kitchen, Anna had talked at length about something, some problem at the butcher's perhaps, until she realised that Hildegard was not listening. Anna guessed where Hildegard had been but kept her horror and her helpless pity to herself. She remained sitting at the table, turning her wedding ring around her finger with only her worry and her sadness for company. Hildegard had gone to bed early, bleeding and twisted, saturated with pain. She was cold to her core, so very cold. Nothing but pain and cold. Then Eleanor had come in and stroked her hair and kissed her, and when her little girl had left, she had lain catatonic in the dark.

When eventually she slept, she dreamed of a raging black maelstrom, spinning madly towards a precipice, beyond which lay a bottomless frozen hell toward which the storm pulled her mercilessly. She saw herself drawn across the barren wasteland between, cowering and stumbling, unable to resist until she reached the brink of the abyss, where a malicious vertigo enticed her on beyond the point where she would fall and be lost forever. Here she stopped, buffeted by the storm, she crouched into a ball on the ground. The spinning in her head stilled. She felt her heart thumping, pounding, then slowing, fading, slowing, stopping. She did not breathe.
Then a jolt, and a gasping in-breath. Her back straightened and her chin lifted, the wet strands of her hair clinging to her face and neck, she stood and looked down into black oblivion. Then she backed away.

The fear that had long accompanied her approach to Prinz Albrecht Strasse was oddly absent the next time she was obliged to report. Hildegard realised that it had in fact been morphing slowly over time, like a seed planted in the earth. It had first grown strong, pervasive roots, and then a determined shoot that burst through the surface as a vibrant plant, the seed's destiny made tangible. Now the adaptation was complete, and the next generation of Hildegard's fear was hate. She observed with detached interest that where the fear had been visceral, the hate was cerebral. The fear, although ever present, had come in tides, ebbing and flowing according to the waxing and waning of her proximity to Gestapo. When it peaked, inside Prinz Albrecht Strasse, it could almost drown her, smothering her until she could barely breathe. Some vile courtesy prevented them from marking her face, but she mapped every deep tender bruise left on her ribs, her hips, her soul. Outside again, battered and retching, gasping for air, there would be a momentary white flash of impotent rage and then that, and the fear would wither and recede.

The hate though, was deeper and more profound. It was there in every cell of her, as much a part of her as her grey eyes and dark hair. It was as fundamental as breathing. Part of it was intellectual, a principled rejection of the Nazi ideology. Part of it she could attribute to what they had driven her to do. Although she did not consider herself religious, she had nonetheless been brought up in the Catholic faith with its belief in the sanctity of human life. The concept of deliberately ending a pregnancy was morally abhorrent to her, it was not a choice she could entertain. But the existence of a child conceived through such brutality was equally unimaginable, when there was already Eleanor, who was the opposite. In the end, she first made the unthinkable choice because there was already Eleanor, who needed shelter, and food and clothes and medicine. Hildegard, like countless mothers before her and countless more to come, had had to concede any remaining trace of the moral high ground to the realities of providing for those already living. It deadened her a little, and the next time deadened her a little more, and the next more still, until the final time, when the cumulative toll dragged her to her nadir.

Hate was the inevitable conclusion, and it gave her both an extraordinary clarity of thought, and an undeniable sense of purpose. The hate created a bubble around her, an invisible shield that separated her from her experiences, so that now, when she entered Prinz Albrecht Strasse, the place and the people in it could not touch her, she was merely an observer. She did not feel the coldness of the place, she was insulated, protected. She watched with detachment, as though from a glass walled viewing gallery, as the Gestapos busily dished out casual cruelties and commonplace abuse, including her own misery. She did not see humiliated victims, now she understood that all of the shame, and all of the guilt, belonged to the tormentors.

It was strange, she pondered about Prinz Albrecht Strasse, how a place so teeming with human life could be so completely devoid of humanity. She saw too the paradoxical truth that it was the jailers who were constrained here. They were restricted within the limits of their ideology, their falsely constructed society. Hildegard did not believe in it and so had no such boundaries. They were powerless to impose them, her mind was free. She no longer considered them a homogenous group of featureless clones. Now the collective guilt was apportioned to each and every one of them, they all had a face and a name and they were all individually accountable.

When she thought of the day she had met the two Gestapos on the train from Charlottenburg, the day of black market coal and strawberries, she considered it the day of her first victory against them. It was a small victory, of which the Gestapos themselves had been unaware, but it was a start.

Chapter 8

The snow had all but gone when Wilhelm came to visit. It had been a year since they had seen him and the visit was doubly exciting because of the great treat that was planned. As the rickety truck pulled up outside the new bungalow, Hildegard was at the door to greet him.

'Papa! How lovely to see you, did you have a good journey?'

'I must say you're looking very well,' said Anna, who had joined Hildegard at the door. Wilhelm kissed his wife and daughter, and bent to pick up Eleanor, who was hiding shyly behind Anna's legs. He held her up in the air, inspecting her.

'You can't be my granddaughter, she's a baby, you're such a big girl!'

Wilhelm said with a smile. Eleanor giggled back at him.

'I am Eleanor, Grandpa!'

'Shall we go inside, instead of standing in the street for all the neighbours to gawp at?' said Anna, aware of the nets twitching at windows. She could imagine what a talking point they would be, dressed in their best clothes, with their hair neat and shining and their shoes carefully polished, greeting this stranger on the doorstep on a saturday morning.

Wilhelm had left early for the long drive east and he was glad to have arrived. There was time only for a quick drink and freshen up before they all went out again together and climbed into the cab of the truck. Anna peered in uncertainly before trusting her good coat to the upholstery, but Wilhelm knew his wife and the cab had been thoroughly cleaned. It was important to him that the trip to Berlin went well, and an argument with Anna would not have been a good start.

Wilhelm had come to Berlin hopeful of securing some foreign trade for his business. He had been able to arrange a meeting with representatives from the Rumanian Embassy to discuss exports and asked Hildegard to accompany him as a secretary and possibly as a translator too. If the Rumanians did not speak German well, she could help by conversing with them in French. They had arranged to meet over lunch at the prestigious Adlon Hotel, and Wilhelm wanted to take the rare opportunity to treat his family. He was busier than he had ever been with work, but still he missed them.

They parked a short walk from the Brandenburg Gate, so the old truck would not give a poor impression of them and walked across the square to the hotel. Anna took Wilhelm's arm and Hildegard held Eleanor's hand, reminding her to be on her best behaviour as she skipped along beside them.

Unscathed, as though protected from the bombs, the hotel was grand and luxurious, with sparkling chandeliers and shell backed sofas upholstered in rich velvet, beneath high vaulted ceilings. It was breathtaking and looking around at the elegant clientele Hildegard was glad she had taken care with her appearance.

She felt a little nervous for the meeting, her French was rusty to say the least, and had never been as fluent as her English in any case. She need not have worried, one of the two Rumanian gentlemen had brought his wife, and the three of them were charming company. To Hildegard's relief, all of them spoke excellent German and conversed easily on every subject, from the design of the hotel, both inside and out, to the music playing in the background, which was not to Hildegard's taste, to the excellent food, which was. They all felt the presence of the black cloud of the war, but withheld permission for it to rain on them by avoiding acknowledging it.

After the meal, they decided to take brandy in the lounge. Eleanor clambered onto one of the stylish sofas and had to be reminded to keep her shoes off the fabric, which was difficult as her feet barely reached the edge of the seat. Anna was deep in conversation with the Rumanian woman, about something to do with embroidery silks, and the men were examining the more technical aspects of Wilhelm's export proposal. Hildegard had little interest in either topic and excused herself to visit the ladies' room. She wound her way through the lounge, and as she reached the corridor to the toilets, a uniformed Gestapo officer on his way out bumped into her.

'Pardon me, Fraulein,' he smiled apologetically and inclined his head politely before returning to his party. He had a pleasant expression on his face but his pale, almost colourless eyes were cold and ominous as the grave. He was unmistakable. Hildegard hurried into the ladies' room and locked herself in a cubicle, leaning her back against the door before daring to breathe. He had not recognised her out of context, but she knew him.

The shock of seeing that Gestapo away from his usual setting in Prinz Albrecht Strasse was short-lived. Hildegard gathered her wits and ventured out of the cubicle. She checked her face in the mirror for telltale signs of panic or anxiety but there were none. It had been a surprise to see him, that was all, although of course she could have expected it. The Adlon was well known as a favoured haunt of Nazi officers, she had just not made the connection before. More of a surprise was that now she knew he was there, she felt only cold curiosity.

She paused at the end of the passage and scanned the room. There he was, sitting at a table with a woman and a little girl not much older than Eleanor. He had pulled the corners of his serviette through his fingers like rabbits' ears and was making her laugh by jumping his hand on and off the table. The woman looked on placidly. She was the model Nazi wife, her hair was pulled neatly back into a blonde bun above the demure neckline of her dress. Hildegard thought she might be pretty, if she smiled.

I wonder if you would look so blandly accepting if you knew what he does at work, she thought. You think he is doing an important job for the Reich, something heroic, something glorious. But he's a coward and a rapist. He picks on defenceless, vulnerable women and he violates them. He tells himself it is justified, but really he does it because he believes himself to be untouchable by any law because he, and his like, are the law.
What would you make of that, I wonder? Myself, I think it's contemptible.
As for you, Gestapo, she thought, turning to the husband, you are neither god nor monster. You are just a weak, spineless man, you hide behind your uniform and follow the goose-stepping crowd. That is your choice, and you are responsible for it. I despise you.
Her eyes wandered across the room to her own party, and she walked gracefully back to join them.

Over the next few weeks, Hildegard spent a lot of time thinking about the Gestapo, both individually and collectively. She knew she was justified in hating them, each of them, all of them, for what they did to her. The hate had crystallised her thoughts as she watched that one in the Hotel Adlon with his family. But the hate had a caustic quality that would rot her from the inside if it remained and leave her a hollowed, brittle shell. It was beginning to taste bitter. She must make use of it somehow, exploit it to fuel her actions. But what was it she wanted to achieve?

She realised too, that day in the Hotel Adlon, that she did not want revenge. She had not been tempted to grab a knife and bury it between the Gestapo's shoulder blades and watch as his colourless eyes turned glassy. Nor had she wanted to hurt his wife or child and avenge herself in that way. The fear had gone, and the flashes of rage had gone with it, replaced by the knowledge of what she must do, and the determination to do it. The crimes that they had committed must be laid bare to the world, and they must be made to answer for them. She simply could not allow them to get away with it. It was not vengeance she sought, but justice.

Chapter 9

As a rule, Hildegard kept herself to herself at work. She valued her privacy and knew that as the English teacher, she was automatically the subject of some suspicion. She was wary when not long after she started, one of her new colleagues approached her in the staff room.

'Mrs O'Reilly? My name's Liam, Liam Mullally. Happy to meet a fellow exile from the Emerald Isle.' He spoke with a lyrical accent and extended his hand to her with a friendly smile.

'Oh, pleased to meet you. It's just Reilly, actually, no O, and it's my husband's family who are originally from Ireland,' Hildegard smiled back.

'I'm sorry, my mistake. By coincidence I've a friend called O'Reilly, you see.'

After that, they would chat occasionally, when their paths crossed at work. They were a similar age, and Hildegard was glad to have, if not a friend exactly, at least a friendly acquaintance and his singsong Irish lilt to listen to.

The buds on the trees were opening with a naive optimism for 1943 when the second significant event of the year happened for Hildegard. In fact, it was she herself that instigated it. In thinking about her dual ambitions of keeping her family safe, and fighting for justice against the Nazi's, she realised that neither would be possible from Berlin. She remembered something Liam had told her at work. He knew someone in a government department that arranged for people to go abroad on information gathering missions for the Reich. On reflection, Hildegard was not entirely sure where Liam's sympathies lay. But that was his business. All she needed was a chance to get away from here, and that would require some legitimate authorisation. Liam had left the Berlitz School the previous summer, but it was easy enough to track him down, he now worked for a radio station. It was time to put her plan into action.

Herr Schuddekopf was in charge of a department called Amt VI D2. It was the England Referat, whose remit included collecting and evaluating information from an array of English publications and periodicals to gain some insight into daily life and morale in England. Hildegard arrived at the appointed time at the offices, which she was relieved to discover were further across town from where she lived and not at Prinz Albrecht Strasse. Inside there was an atheneum air of scholarly endeavour, which she would have found comforting, had she not been acutely aware that Amt VI D2 was a division of the RSHA, just like the Gestapo.

A secretary showed her into an office whose walls were lined with shelves on the brink of a paper avalanche. A plaque among the detritus on the desk identified Herr Doctor O E Schuddekopf. Doctor of what? wondered Hildegard. He looked like a studious man, or maybe just a student, with his too big suit hanging awkwardly on his slight frame. He moved constantly, like a bird searching for seeds. He took small steps this way and that, scanning through thick round wire-rimmed spectacles the array of books and papers on every available surface. He looked and then, preoccupied, immediately forgot what he saw and was obliged to look again. Eventually, his field of vision included Hildegard, waiting patiently just inside the door and he stopped still and blinked at her.

'Come in, come in. Sit down.' It was an enthusiastically issued invitation, not a blunt order. He sat opposite with his hands in his lap, as though resting on a valued book, leaning forward slightly and staring intently at her, still blinking through his thick glasses. Hildegard smiled politely, although her heart was racing. It was imperative that this meeting went well.

'Hildegard Reilly,' she prompted.

'Yes! Yes, I remember, you're English, aren't you? Dr Schuddekopf,' he extended his hand.

'Yes.' Hildegard had been expecting something like a Gestapo, but Dr Schuddekopf was not in uniform, he used no title of military rank, he did not even wear a party badge. He was about as far from her experience of Gestapos as it was possible to be and she was not sure what to make of him. Her instincts told her that he bore her no malice, but still, she was cautious.

'So, I gather you think we can help each other?' He had remembered why the meeting had been arranged, and he conscientiously gave her his full attention. 'Tell me your circumstances, Mrs Reilly.'

'Well, I teach English, at the Berlitz School. We live just out of town, we moved recently from rooms in a building behind the Zeughaus. The bombing, you know,' she shrugged.

'We?'

'My mother, and my daughter also.'

'How old is your daughter?'

'She's four.'

'And what of your husband?'

'You might say we are separated. He went to England, and we were supposed to follow him, but then the war began and we couldn't. I haven't heard from him since.' A lot of information given, but all of it already known to the authorities.

'Nothing? For more than three years? No, well, I suppose it has not been possible,' he answered his own question.

Hildegard shook her head. The grief she had felt at Bern's absence had defined her at the start. Back then, she had thought of herself as Hildegard, whose husband is not here. Over the long, silent years since, other things, more practical, more urgent, had occupied her thoughts, and Bern was pushed back until he almost fell from them altogether. She wondered vaguely whether he was still alive. If anything had happened to him, how would she know? It occurred to her that it was not the most important thing to her anymore. If he had made any effort to help them from England, it had not been successful and anyway, she could not be sure that he had even tried. He had uselessly wished her luck when the war started. But he might prove useful now. Sometimes you have to make your own luck. She took a deep breath.

'I believe my husband is a relative of Sir Hughe Knatchbull-Hugessen, who is the British Ambassador in Turkey.'

Hildegard could feel her heart pounding against her ribs at telling so audacious a lie, but she pressed on. 'I wondered, with such a connection and being British now myself of course, if I might be able to usefully join an English ex-patriate community in that country?'

There, she had said it. She had half expected him to laugh, but on the contrary, Schuddekopf regarded her thoughtfully.

'That could indeed be useful,' he said eventually. 'I would need to discuss it with my colleague Matysiak in the Turkey Referat. Turkey remains a neutral state, of course, but would be a most desirable ally. In any case, it hosts a unique mix of international guests. You would have some legitimacy there as a British subject and fellow ex-patriate, and presumably one with some standing, given your connection to the Ambassador. That position could be a most interesting source of information. If my colleague agrees, arrangements can be made very quickly.'

Hildegard held her breath, she could hardly believe he was taking her proposal seriously.

'What will your family do, if you leave Berlin, is there somewhere they could go?'

'Well, there are aunts, yes, they could go to one of my mother's sisters, in the country.'

The price to pay for leaving Berlin was leaving Eleanor, and the cost of separation was high, she already knew that. But this was the only solution she could think of that would both take Eleanor and Anna to relative safety and satisfy her own need to act.

'All right,' he said, 'I will see what can be arranged,' then, regarding her thoughtfully added, 'I suppose your life here has been, difficult, of late?'

'Yes,' she said quietly, 'I have to report, of course.'

He understood the implications of reporting for a woman in Hildegard's position, and it sickened him.

'You would still be required to report, of course, any information that you discover. But in a neutral country, the Nazis are not in charge, do you see? They are not the law.'

There was a kindness in his tone, and Hildegard was grateful for his compassion. He had referred to the Nazis as "they", not "we".

'You,' she began tentatively, 'forgive me for asking, but you do not wear a party badge?'

'No,' he leaned back in his chair, considering his answer. 'I am not a member of the party. I'm not politically motivated at all, really. I do have strong personal convictions, though. Not religious exactly, more, humanitarian, and that is largely what guides me.'

He looked at her candidly and an unspoken understanding passed between them. 'Goodness knows how I ended up in this job. I expect someone will notice at some point, and make me wear a uniform,' he smiled, a small, rueful smile. 'I assume that you are not a member of the party either?'

Hildegard wondered if he was joking.

'No,' she said evenly, 'no I'm not.'

Very much not. Quite the opposite.

They talked a while longer, agreeing a plan, but Hildegard was not concerned at that moment with the details. She recognised that here was an opportunity, a precious chance and she must not waste it. They shook hands as she was leaving, sealing the deal. 'Might I ask why, Dr. Schuddekopf? Why are you doing this for me?'

'Substantively, you are going on a mission for the Reich, remember that. But for myself, remember what else I told you. It is my convictions that compel me.'

Hildegard nodded, mine too, Dr Schuddekopf. He returned her smile with warmth. 'And it's Otto, Otto-Ernst.'

Earnest indeed, thought Hildegard.

Chapter 10

The third significant event of 1943, both catastrophic and catalytic, occurred some weeks later, when the trees were sagging in the torpid air, weighed down by their gorgeous leaves.

In late July and early August the Allies bombed Hamburg without mercy, killing countless thousands of people. Many people died under the relentless direct hits, and more still in the hellish fire storms caused by the phosphorus bombs. The intense heat from the fires sucked all the oxygen from the air causing winds like mighty hurricanes to form. The winds fed the inferno sucking everything, even animals and people, irresistibly into the insatiable flames.

On the last night of July, Allied planes dropped leaflets over Berlin, warning women and children to leave immediately, just as they had over Hamburg before the bombing there, causing alarm throughout the city that Berlin would be next. The order was given to evacuate all of the children, and any women not employed in defence work.

The plans for Anna and Eleanor to go to Anna's sister in the country were abandoned. The further away they could get, the quicker, the better. Hildegard managed to secure places for her mother and daughter on the Mutter und Kinder transport out of

Berlin. They would join the river of evacuees travelling south, to be billeted for the foreseeable future in the mountains of Silesia, near the Czech border.

There was chaos at the station when the time came to leave. The crowd murmurated like starlings, confounding its own intent to flee. There were hundreds of women and children boarding trains out of Berlin, and at least as many more pouring in from Hamburg. The stories they brought with them were terrifying, and only fueled the compulsion to escape before the same horror reached Berlin. Hildegard tried not to be drawn into the general state of hysteria, but it was hard to remain calm in such an atmosphere. She held Eleanor's hand tightly and lead them through the throng to the train, forcing a smile for Eleanor's sake.

'You are going on such an adventure, it will be exciting! You and Grandma must write and tell me all about it.' Hildegard had knelt to be at Eleanor's level.

'I wish you were coming too, Mummy,' the corners of Eleanor's mouth turned down and her eyes were wide and tear-filled. Her little arms clung tightly around Hildegard's neck.

'I know, sweetheart, I do too. But I have to go to work. Grandma will take the best care of you, and I'm sure it won't be for very long.'

Hildegard glanced up at Anna and saw her purse her lips at the white lie, but what else could she do? Her instinct was to comfort her daughter, surely Anna could understand that.

Still fighting back tears Hildegard held Eleanor's small slight body close to her and breathed in the smell of her to seal in her memory. The guard's call for passengers to board pulled them apart and Hildegard put Eleanor's hand in Anna's. The two women embraced each other briefly and then Hildegard watched Anna and Eleanor board the train and settle in their seats without her.

Since this plan had been hatched, Hildegard had battled her conflicting emotions. She was committed to the path she had chosen for herself and she knew that they must leave Berlin, that

Anna and Eleanor would be safer in the south, but there were moments of panic, final waverings before it was too late. What if she were wrong? How could she be sure this was the safest option for them? What if the train were bombed on the way? They had a long journey ahead of them and no certainty at all about either that or where they would end up. How could it be right for a mother to send her little girl away from her through a war? Interspersed with the worry, and harder to admit, even to herself, there was guilt. Hildegard felt guilty for not going with them, guilty for consigning them to an unknown fate, guilty for relinquishing responsibility for Eleanor and worst of all, she felt guilty for the relief of their departure.

She put her hand to the window as though to hold them there, but a whistle blew and she watched the train pull away from the platform, tearing her heart from her chest as it went. Her mother and her daughter waved bravely through the window. This was surely their best chance, perhaps their only chance to stay safe. She had to let them go. Hildegard waved back, until the train disappeared from view

Chapter 11

Silesia, August 1943

A long journey on an overcrowded train delivered them, along with dozens of other women and children, to a town called Hirschberg. Eleanor had never seen mountains before, and she stared transfixed at the high rolling ridge of the Silesian range looming over them. There was no time for wonderment when the train stopped though, as they were briskly herded onto buses or the backs of trucks, or horse-drawn carts that would transport them to their billets.

Anna and Eleanor were allocated to an isolated smallholding at the foot of the mountains. A surly old man lived there with his quiet, stern-faced wife, their fourteen year old grandson, a cow and a pig. Immediately, Eleanor did not like the place, she whispered to Anna that it made her feel afraid, like they shouldn't really be there.

'We'll soon get used to it,' Anna told her, 'they don't let us choose where stay, we go where we are put and we were put here, so we'll just have to make the best of it. It's very good of these people to share their home with us. Let's be polite guests, shall we?'

Eleanor could not settle at the farm. She spent most of the first few days wandering listlessly around the yard, dragging her doll by the hand behind her. At the far end of the yard there was a little barn, where the old woman tied the cow for milking. Eleanor was not allowed to go into the barn in case she got trampled, but she took to standing in the doorway and looking in. Sometimes the cow would lift her head, still chewing lazily, and rest her long-lashed, liquid brown eyes on Eleanor. Despite her size, the cow seemed a gentle creature, and Eleanor thought she must be kind to give up her milk every day. The still warm raw milk they had for breakfast was the best thing about this place.

Anna concentrated on keeping her granddaughter occupied, both to pass the time and to take her mind off missing her mother. It seemed like the little girl had hardly spoken since they left Berlin, except to ask when they would see Mummy, and every time she did felt like another stone weighing down Anna's heart just a little more. She twisted her wedding ring, hoping the separation would get easier for Eleanor with time.

Not many days after they arrived, the teenage boy caught Eleanor leaning against the doorframe of the barn, watching the cow.

'You like her, don't you?'

Eleanor jumped, she had not heard him approach. She nodded, warily.

'How would you like to ride her, then? Like a cowboy?'

With one swoop, he lifted her in both hands and carried her into the barn, placing her none too carefully astride the startled cow's back.

'No! Please put me down!' Eleanor wailed, her eyes wide. She felt around but there was nothing on the cow's neck for her to hold on to. The cow lifted her head and shifted her feet, which sent a ripple across her mighty shoulders. She had seemed a gentle creature from the doorway, but from her back she was monstrous. 'Put me down!' pleaded Eleanor again, in panic. But the boy just laughed.

'No! You're a cowboy now, you can ride the cow, until she bucks you off, that is. Let's have a rodeo, Cowboy!'

'Please!' wailed Eleanor.

There was a dull thud, as the flat of the woman's hand connected with the back of the boy's head.

'What are you doing, you idiot? Don't you know what that cow is worth?'

She lifted Eleanor off briskly and set her down outside the barn, turning immediately back to soothe her precious animal. The boy stood in the middle of the yard, rubbing the back of his head. Eleanor took a deep breath and marched straight up to him.

'That was mean,' she said. He blinked at her, speechless. He could have expected the reprimand from his grandmother, but not this, from a four year old. He opened his mouth to say something, but Eleanor had not finished.

'And I,' she informed him, 'am a girl.'

She stomped furiously toward the house, from where Anna had witnessed the entire episode. She was as surprised as the boy by Eleanor's defiance, but she was also impressed by her granddaughter's display of character. Perhaps she will be alright after all, she thought. Anna raised her eyebrows at the boy, who sloped off, avoiding both the house and the barn.

Rules or no rules, thought Anna, we will not be staying here. That afternoon, she had a very serious conversation with the billeting officer.

•

Chapter 12

Berlin, September 1943

After Anna and Eleanor left on the Mutter und Kinder transport, Hildegard remained in Berlin for a few weeks more. Toward the end of August came the heaviest air raid on the city to date, and she was agitated with impatience to leave. She gave her notice at the Berlitz School and planned one final task to complete on her last day.

Reinhardt had had little of note to report on recently, even his great hero Rommel had failed to provide him with any real successes to crow about. Italy had abandoned the Axis, and Allied troops were advancing in that country from the south. The German army held its ground in the north and in early September occupied Rome, the most prestigious consolation possible for losing control of the south. Reinhardt chose to interpret this news as a resounding victory and relished announcing it to Hildegard in his usual manner at the end of the lesson. He stood by her desk and confidently predicted, in

German, how the Wehrmacht would stand firm in Rome and soon progress south once more, reclaiming what was lost to them.

Instead of her rote response, the threadbare reminder to speak only English in her classroom, Hildegard stood up and faced him squarely, tilting her chin up to address him.

'The Wehrmacht may progress, or they may not, Reinhardt, we shall have to wait and see. One thing is certain, and that is that I have an important job to do for the war effort, and I am leaving immediately to pursue it. You might want to consider what your own contribution is. Anyway, good luck with your studies, you certainly need it. Goodbye Reinhardt. Heil Hitler.'

The precise fluency with which she delivered this speech in her first language left him gaping speechless at the door, which had clicked gently closed behind her.

The following day Hildegard was at the railway station again, this time to start a journey of her own.

Chapter 13

Kiesewald, September 1943

Anna and Eleanor's second lodgings suited them far better than the first. It was a house in the centre of a small village called Kiesewald, a little further up the slope. The buildings in this village were uniform in shape, each house crouched under a steeply pitched roof which finished low over the ground floor to avoid too heavy a build-up of the inevitable winter snow. The house where they were to stay was unique both in size, in happier times it was run as a bed and breakfast by Mrs Braun and her two daughters, and in atmosphere, because it contained the three of them.

It was late afternoon when the new guests arrived. Anna knocked, with some trepidation after their first experience, but she need not have worried.
'Come in, come in, you must be exhausted!' Mrs Braun opened the door wide and ushered them to the table and poured them

each a glass of cool fresh water. 'Girls, take our guests bags up to their room.'

Anna and Eleanor had not travelled far from the farm, but in the late summer heat they were grateful for the drink and even more so for the welcome. Looking around the kitchen, Anna could see that this was a room in which people cooked and cleaned and worked and ate and talked and listened. It was a room where a family lived.

That evening over a delicious peasant stew Anna told them the story of the incident with the boy and the cow which had caused them to leave their previous lodgings.

'You should have seen her, standing there with her hands on her hips, absolutely furious with him! I think he was more scared of little Eleanor than he was of his grandmother.'

'Quite right too!' laughed Mrs Braun, 'I wish I had seen it. It sounds like you stood up to the bully magnificently, brave girl.'

Eleanor smiled shyly and wriggled a little in her seat.

'I heard a story in the village today,' Mrs Braun continued, still smiling, 'one of our neighbours has been arrested.'

'Gosh, that's not funny. Who is it?' asked Erika, the elder daughter.

'Max, you know, lives down at the bottom of the village. They got him for smuggling goods across the border.'

'I see him in the mornings, Mum,' said Erika with a furrowed brow, 'he just pushes an empty wheelbarrow around, there's never anything in it. What on earth do they think he's been smuggling?'

Mrs Braun looked around the table with a twinkle in her eyes.

'Wheelbarrows!'

Everyone laughed.

'Apparently, he has been crossing the border every morning with an empty wheelbarrow, and then returning in the afternoon when the guard has changed, with nothing at all. Quite clever, really. And who would have thought there was such an untapped market?'

A little later the younger daughter, Hedda, got up to refill the pitcher. Returning to the table, she crouched behind her mother, pretending to wipe a spill on the floor. With a conspiratorial wink at Eleanor, she tied her mother's apron strings to her chair. As they finished eating there was a knock on the door, and Mrs Braun rose to answer it. The chair rose with her, and the three of them dissolved in fits of laughter. Eleanor giggled and then looked at Anna in case she disapproved, but Anna was laughing. She was enjoying the joke as much as any of them, but more than that, she was relieved to see Eleanor happy.

The following morning, the whole family took Anna and Eleanor on a tour of the garden, which was brief as it consisted only of a yard, much smaller than the one at the farm, and a patch of scrubby grass, with a little wooden hut to the side where two goats were tethered.

'Is that a castle up there? A golden castle?' Eleanor asked. She was looking across the valley at a building even higher up, its windows dazzling in the morning sun.

'It's a ski lodge,' Mrs Braun told her. 'Not that anyone's skiing much at the moment. Behind it, over that mountain, that's the Protektorat. And over in that direction is Poland. There's a saying here that there's a uniform in every Silesian's closet.'

'Why is there?' asked Eleanor.

'Well, when you live this close to so many borders, there's always somebody wanting a fight.'

Hedda crouched next to Eleanor and pointed to the mountain.

'You see those two black holes in the hill, just below the ski lodge? A plane flew in to one of them and disappeared completely! No-one has found any trace of it since,' she said, wiggling her fingers spookily, her voice trailing off mysteriously.

'That's because it didn't happen,' said Erika, rolling her eyes.

'They're not holes, they're snow pits. They're just part of the mountain, they soon fill up when the winter comes, you'll see,' said Mrs Braun, 'and the missing plane is a mountain myth. That's enough of your tall stories, Hedda, now go and milk the goat. Show little Eleanor how you do it.'

Rural life was very different from the city Eleanor had known up until then. She was almost five years old, and too small to manage most of the domestic tasks, like milking the goat or chopping the wood, but she would keep the girls company as they went about their chores. There was no radio here, so Eleanor sang her favourite song instead.

'La la la la la la la,
 La la Lili Marleen'

'I know that song, "Lili Marleen",' said Hedda. 'It's, I can't remember, do you know who the singer is?'

'Lale Andersen,' said Eleanor, pleased with herself for knowing the answer.

'Lala?' said Hedda, 'Doesn't she know the words either?'

Hedda thought her own joke was hilarious and delighted in sharing it at lunchtime when she told everyone at the table. Eleanor still did not understand.

Later that afternoon, while Eleanor was out with Hedda, Anna wandered into the kitchen. Mrs Braun was starting to cook the evening meal, so she offered to help.

'There's not much to do, to be honest. But if you're any good with a needle, there's a pile of mending I haven't got around to over there.'

Anna picked up the sewing basket, glad to be of use.

'We're really very grateful to you for having us, Mrs Braun. It is lovely to be here,' she said as she settled herself near the window.

'You're very welcome, both of you. Especially if you do the sewing, I'm useless at it,' Mrs Braun said with a smile, 'And please, call me Maria.'

'I'm Anna.' She warmed to this woman who had opened her home to them with such generosity.

'Your little Eleanor is a sweetheart,' said Maria.

'She is. Your daughter seems to have taken her under her wing, I hope she doesn't mind her tagging along.'

'Not at all. I only hope she doesn't lead her into any mischief, Hedda can be a bit of a handful at times,' Maria rolled her eyes, but her voice was full of affection for her younger child.

'My daughter, Eleanor's mother, is the same. She was always such a willful child. My husband would say she was spirited. Difficult, I would say.' Anna said ruefully. Maria stopped chopping and turned to her.

'Well,' she said gently, 'better a spirited girl than one that can't stand up for herself, don't you think? And in my experience, they tend to be the more resourceful ones too.'

'Perhaps you're right,' Anna conceded. Funny how a stranger seemed to be more insightful about her daughter than she was herself. It had not occurred to her that what she considered a shortcoming, Hildegard's stubborn independence, might actually be a saving grace.

Chapter 14

Istanbul, September 1943

After rattling doggedly through the night the train from Sofia drew in to Sirkeci station at Istanbul. The city's name alone conjured mystical images in Hildegard's daydreams, she had long imagined it would be thrilling to arrive in such an exotic place as this. The reality was rather more prosaic. The station was as busy as any and Hildegard was bustled along with the crowd across the marble-floored, stained glass-lit waiting area that she had no time to admire, and out onto an already baking street. She felt tired, dusty and lousy, and she wanted a bath. A fellow traveller had recommended a hotel where she could book in just for a bath and breakfast and she gratefully sank into the back seat of a taxi to follow his advice.

The Park Hotel was an impressive, stucco'ed building, in the art deco style. It was high on a hill with spectacular views from the terrace of the city and the Bosphorus below. Across the fork in the water she could see ancient domes and minarets that she would later learn belonged to the Blue Mosque, the Agia Sofia and the Topkapi Palace, the landmarks of old Constantinople. Taking a breath, Hildegard squared her shoulders, lifted her chin and walked confidently up the steps as the taxi driver handed her suitcase and hatbox to a bellhop. She was glad of the hatbox, it was the luggage of a lady, a status symbol, one of the props of her role and a little giver of confidence. Before her meeting with Schuddekopf in Berlin, she had taken pains to transform into a more worldly-wise version of herself, partly as persuasive argument for being entrusted with a grown-up mission, and partly as a mask to hide behind, a shield for self-protection.

She had enrolled Anna in making adjustments to her wardrobe, a girlish peter pan collar removed so a neckline revealed her collarbones, a slightly narrower skirt, a more defined waist. Anna had tutted disapprovingly, but stitched miracles, as was her gift.

In Berlin, Hildegard had walked past the posters exhorting women not to wear make-up and not to smoke, but to stay at home and raise a brood of good, Aryan children. Not this woman, she thought, as she stepped inside the Kaufhaus Des Westens, the best department store in the city. She invested a small fortune in an arsenal for her mission, a fluted gold tube of red lipstick, a short, amber cigarette holder, octagonal in cross-section and very stylish, and a silver powder compact with a green enameled lid that shut with a satisfying snap.

Having some time to spare, Hildegard had indulged herself for a while, wandering around the shop, enjoying looking at the rare luxuries on display. She caught sight of a fashionable young woman walking toward her. She watched her for a moment, intrigued and a little in awe of the woman's poise and self-assurance. She wore a well-cut suit and a slick of red lipstick and her shiny dark curls were fashionably pinned. The woman gazed back at Hildegard with clear grey eyes and a confident smile, and Hildegard had thought, as she turned away from the tall shop mirror, that is who I must be, the person I now appear to be to all the world. Real, but not real.

Two hours later, bathed, breakfasted and dressed in freshly de-loused clothes, Hildegard walked from the Istanbul Park Hotel to the German Consulate next door. The reception clerk looked down his nose at her, provoking her to glare back defiantly, determined that her reality in Istanbul would not match her reality in Berlin. He sniffed and gave her a curt instruction to wait as he stalked off down a corridor. A few minutes later he returned and summoned her to follow him back along the corridor, to a door at the end, the entrance to the lair of Vice-Consul Bruno Wolff. The clerk knocked and headed back to his station without waiting for a response, leaving Hildegard alone in the gloomy grey corridor. Eventually a voice within said 'Kommen Sie.'

Hildegard stepped inside a large sepia toned corner office. There were windows on adjacent sides, with wide wooden shutters at a slant that sliced the sunlight into precise parallel bars on the floor. It was a sombre place, sparsely furnished with dark wood and cracked brown leather pieces, if they held any value it was utilitarian rather than aesthetic. Behind the substantial double pedestal desk a man sat studying a document, making peevish annotations in the margins in blue ink. He glanced up at her and wordlessly indicated the chair opposite him with the top of his pen before resuming his task. Hildegard perched on the chair and observed him. He was perhaps in his mid-thirties, dark and serious looking, wearing a pinstriped business suit with a party badge in the lapel. There was a framed photo of a woman and a little girl on the desk, which he turned toward himself when he noticed Hildegard looking at it. With an irritated frown, he screwed the cap onto his pen and tucked the document into a folder.

'Frau Reilly. Just arrived from Berlin.' He stated flatly, turning his attention to her at last.

'Yes,' said Hildegard steadily. There was a silence which she resisted filling.

'Hauptsturmbahnfuhrer Matysiak informed me he had sent you. He thinks you will serve some purpose here, but I have my doubts.'

Hildegard sat very still and held his gaze, remembering Schuddekopf's words, the Nazis are not the law in Istanbul. Wolff exhaled impatiently.

'Well, we'll see. You have your German papers and your marriage certificate?'

'Yes'

'Your orders are to present yourself at the British Consulate and request a British passport, as is your right. Do you have work arranged?'

'Yes, at a place called Taksim's Casino. An agency…'

'I know Taksim's,' he interrupted her. 'Many ex-patriates frequent it. You will do your best to talk to British and Americans there, and also at the British Consulate. Any information you hear, you will report to me. I will inform you when to report, and I will judge if what you learn is useful or not.'

'Understood.'

With a curt "Heil Hitler" she was dismissed.

It was late morning as Hildegard left the German Consulate and the city heat was heavy. Relieved to have that place and all it represented behind her, she lifted her face to the sky and took a deep slow breath in and exhaled, purging herself of its toxic atmosphere. Opening her eyes, she noticed how beautiful the buildings opposite were. A row of elegant townhouses, tall windows ornamented with wrought iron balconies, almost Parisien, some almost derelict. She noticed too the trees that lined the road. They cast a dappled shade along the wide boulevard, a monochrome approximation of the pattern of their bark and Hildegard recognised her old affinity with pleasure.

She had almost stopped seeing the trees in Berlin, they had cycled through patience, optimism, exuberance, splendour, slow, regretful detachment and back to sleeping patience more than once without her. Here, the leaves were contentedly basking in the sun, fading summer green and whispering gently in anticipation of their autumn colours. She walked back past the Park Hotel, where she had left her luggage with the concierge, and on toward the British Consulate, feeling the warmth and the trees infusing life into her veins.

Approaching the British Consulate, Hildegard saw a white stone Italianate building, surrounded by beautiful gardens, and thought it far more elegant than its German counterpart, the stolid red brick block she had just left. She walked up the wide stone steps to tall double doors flanked by pink oleanders and stepped inside. Hildegard presented her papers to the clerk, had he said his name was Whitehead? Whittall? She did not quite catch which. He politely invited her to a small anonymous side office.

'So, Mrs Reilly, if I understand correctly, you are German? German birth certificate, born in Köln, that's Cologne, correct? And German travel documents. You have arrived here from Sofia, I see?'

'Yes.'

Schuddekopf had furnished her with an exit permit to leave Germany, and her father's friends in the Rumanian Embassy in Berlin had kindly provided a visa so that Hildegard could travel via their country and several others, either collaborative or occupied, to get to Turkey.

'But I am British now, here, my marriage certificate. My husband is British, we married in Berkshire, in 1937.' She understood that he was just doing his job, but she was impatient to get to the point of her being here.

'And where is your husband?'

'In England, I think. Quite honestly, I don't know.'

"Hmmm." He raised a sceptical eyebrow. 'Will you be registering with the German Consulate here too?'

'Yes.' At last. 'Actually, I've already been there.' Hildegard looked directly into the clerk's eyes. She could see that he was not sure what to make of her, but this was her opportunity, and she would not let it drift past. She took a deep breath and a huge leap of faith.

'They sent me here. They said I should apply for a British passport, and try to find out any information, and then report back to them.'

The clerk looked incredulous. He shook his head slowly, as though rolling her words around in his mind would rearrange them into an order that made sense.

'And you are telling me this because...?' he said uncertainly.

Now to propose the mission she had engineered, the important work for the war effort about which she had told Reinhardt. She had meant, of course, the Allied war effort, not the Axis, as he had assumed. Hildegard leaned toward the clerk and enunciated each word very clearly, so as not to be misunderstood.

'I am telling you this, because I need to know what exactly it is that you would like me to tell them,' she said.

The clock on the wall ticked.

'Mrs. Reilly, would you like to wait in the Palm Court, while I have your papers checked?'

She followed him across the corridor, where he left her in a central atrium, bright with light from three floors of tall windows and a glass lantern roof high above. The clerk vanished through a door at one end and Hildegard waited. It was cool, despite the glass, the marble floor and large potted palms made a secret oasis of the space. Still she waited, patient, if a little nervous. Eventually, the clerk reappeared.

'Your, ahem,' he cleared his throat, 'somewhat unusual, circumstances will be considered,' he informed her.

'What does that mean?' she asked.

'Good day, Mrs Reilly.' He was showing her out through the lobby. 'I assure you of our best attention to your passport application, and your other information.' Hildegard was paying attention, but there was not so much as a hint of what he thought about what she had told him. 'We will be in touch.'

Once again she was dismissed, this time with a cordial handshake.

Chapter 15

A longer stay at the Park Hotel was beyond Hildegard's means, so she checked into a cheaper establishment that would do until she could find a flat to rent. After unpacking her luggage, she spent the late afternoon wandering around the area, finding her bearings, relishing her freedom. It seemed to Hildegard that Istanbul was a city full of strays. Cats, dogs, people, each with a story, a reason they were here. Each, including herself, finding a way to survive. She watched a cat, apparently trapped on a sill behind an ornate metal window grille, as it wove itself between the bars, stepped delicately onto a curlicue and leapt effortlessly up to a portico above a door. You weren't trapped at all, she thought, once you chose not to be.

Within a couple of weeks, Hildegard had found and settled into a new home in a steep cobbled street at the side of the German Consulate. It was in a purpose-built apartment block, square, functional and featureless, and consisted of two rooms, with a tiny kitchen and a bathroom. The unremarkable interior was more than compensated by the view of the Bosphorus. The whole place would rattle alarmingly during the frequent earth tremors, but before long they became tolerable and eventually she barely noticed them.

It was a short walk from the apartment to Hildegard's new place of work, up the steep hill alongside the German Consulate, onto the boulevard where the tall townhouses opposite always demanded she look up. She rounded the corner of Taksim Square, and walked into the gardens, neat and well-tended, newly planted with trees yet too small to offer any shade.

She thought, at first, that the building was a cinema, or some similar, banal municipal provision. She had walked straight it past more than once. When she realised it was the place she was looking for and pushed open the door, some kind of magic happened. Immediately she was in the mysterious Orient, where an exotic middle-eastern cabaret danced to live music, and the background hum was a low babel of customers enjoying fine food at the tables surrounding the dance floor, and drinking apparently infinite amounts of alcohol.

She found the owner, a bear-like White Russian, surveying his domain from behind the bar. Her job would be to serve drinks and socialise with the customers and there were many of them, representatives of the numerous nationalities in the Istanbul melting pot. The Russian knew them all. Hildegard would start straight away and should be prepared for some late nights as talking and dancing here often continued into the small hours of the morning.

Wolff would come in, from time to time, with some of his friends. Hildegard had not been surprised to learn that although his official title was Vice-Consul, he was actually head of the Sicherheitsdeinst, or SD, in Istanbul. The Gestapo could not operate beyond the borders of the Reich, so abroad, they used the cover of this, their sister agency instead.

A Wolff in wolf's clothing, she thought warily, cut from the same cloth as Gestapo. He rarely acknowledged her in the Casino, but she knew he was watching.

Wolff had not been at Taksim's on this particular evening, but plenty of other people had and near to closing time Hildegard's feet were aching. She was longing for her bath which, despite the sometimes reluctant plumbing, still felt like an indescribable luxury when she remembered the washstand in the attics in Berlin. She looked around the Casino to see if it was likely any of the regular late stayers would keep her there after hours.

'Hey Sam, face any firing squads lately?' she heard the White Russian address a man at the far end of the bar. She had not noticed him before, nor did she recognise him. The Russian saw her looking and jerked his thumb at the man.

'This, only guy I ever met who face firing squad and live to tell story.' He shuffled off toward the kitchen, chuckling to himself, leaving an empty space between Hildegard and the stranger.

'Hello, I'm Hildegard,' she said, taking a few steps toward him.

'Sam Brewer,' he offered his hand.

He was American, she could tell from his accent although it was not pronounced. He was average height, average build, brown hair, blue eyes, average grey suit. An everyman. Not surprising she had not noticed him really. But now that she looked, there was something about him, an openness in his face, that she was drawn to.

'Did you really face a firing squad?' she was intrigued.

'Yes, Ma'am.'

'How, I mean, what happened?'

'Oh, well, it was a couple of years ago, in Yugoslavia. I'm a newspaper man, Chicago Tribune.'

A journalist. Probably useful not to stand out in a crowd then. He was an observer, a narrator, a storyteller but not a lead actor.

'I see. Go on.'

'Belgrade was being bombed, so I travelled there to cover the story. Or at least as near as I could, the train stopped about ten miles out of the city, it was a long walk in.'

She picked up a cloth to polish some glasses but she was listening intently.

'There were German dive bombers wheeling like flocks of starlings over the city - wait, your name's Hildegard? Are you German? You don't sound German.'

'British,' said Hildegard crisply. Sam looked at her quizzically. 'Really I am. It's a long story, you first.'

After the briefest pause, when Sam seemed to be making a mental note to return to what she had said, he continued.

'Alright. As the sun went down there was a great black cloud over the city, which was burning orange, and I headed for it, with a forty-pound pack on my back and carrying my typewriter. There were people streaming the other way, with what of their possessions they could carry, but no-one going my way. I got stopped for half an hour at a military checkpoint while they examined my passport. It was dark by the time I got to Belgrade. There were fires everywhere, it looked like a corner of hell.'

He took a sip of his vodka. Hildegard was reminded of the bombed, burning streets of Berlin by those he described in Belgrade. She nodded her understanding, wanting to hear more.

'I found the British Legation, but there was nobody there. The Reuters office was bombed out, same for the American Minister's residence. By about ten o'clock that night, I'd got as far as the Regent Prince Paul's Palace when I was stopped again, this time by a band of eight vigilante Serbs, all with shotguns or pistols.'

'Chetniks?' Hildegard asked.

'I guess so, although back then the Yugoslav resistance under Mihailović was just getting started. One of them wanted to shoot me there and then, but the others said they should search me first. So in the glare of the fire they dumped my knapsack and my typewriter on the pavement, while I watched with my hands in the air and a shotgun in my back. They found a coil of wire for typewriter repairs, a spare flashlight battery and a pair of boots.'

'I don't follow, what was wrong with that?' asked Hildegard.

'Obviously the wire was a radio antenna, the battery and the typewriter were a radio transmitter and the boots, well, the boots were German army issue.'

'Were they?' Hildegard was shocked. No wonder he had found himself in trouble.

'No,' Sam laughed, 'but they couldn't make any sense of my passport either, I think they were illiterate, they thought it was forged. So there was all the evidence they needed. I was definitely a spy.'

'So they were going to shoot you?' Despite Sam's grin, Hildegard was horrified.

'It looked that way. But just at that moment, an army major drove by in the darkness. They called out to him "Parachutist, radio apparatus". He stopped, but he wouldn't listen to anything I said, or even look at my papers. Instead he had me bundled into a second car with two guards.'

'They kidnapped you and held you hostage!' Hildegard gasped. She was completely absorbed in the drama of his story, and it amused him.

'I guess they did,' he agreed. 'The bombers began their night attack on Belgrade and we drove away from the city and around the countryside for hours. We stopped at intervals for the major to look over the roadside, I thought he was looking for a convenient place to leave me, you know, as a corpse. Eventually, around six in the morning, we parked in a cherry orchard by the Danube. He told the guards that he would deal with me at nine o'clock, and then he went to sleep in the back of his car.'

'Gosh. You had three hours to live? Or to escape! What happened next?'

'I decided it was time to put up more of an argument and spent a good part of that time telling my guards, who fortunately spoke French, that I must be released to do my work or there would be a lot of explaining for the Major to do.'

'Did that work?'

'Not really. They weren't impressed. Then, just before nine o'clock a pair of Serb newspaper men whose car had broken down nearby, came to take a look at the "spy". One of them discovered that I knew some of his friends. He tried to intercede on my behalf.'

'Did *that* work?' Hildegard could not imagine how he had survived.

'Not at all. The Major had him arrested too and put under guard along with me.'

'Oh dear. So how did you, well, not get shot?'

'Luckily for me, a third Serb newspaper man came along, to rescue his colleague. This guy was an editor, and a Colonel in the army reserve, and a friend of the Major. He thought I had an honest face and talked the Major into letting me go.'

'Lucky for you indeed,' said Hildegard.

'Yeah.' He sighed and went on, more serious now. 'There was a lot of fear there because of the attack on the city. Every foreigner was a spy, everyone's papers were forgeries, everyone suspected everyone else of being a "fifth columnist". There was no sense of proportion.'

'That's true of a lot of places.' Again, Hildegard was thinking of Berlin. 'What's a "fifth columnist"?'

'Someone who's a member of a hidden opposition group. They're spies and subversives, ready to rise up come the liberation. Or the invasion, depending whose side you're on. So named in the Spanish Civil War.'

'I suppose you were a newspaper man there, too?' Hildegard said.

'Yes, Ma'am,' he said, grinning like a boy caught out. He finished his drink and by then Hildegard had decided he was definitely neither average nor an everyman. He talked easily but with no ego, telling his story with genuine interest in the events, despite the potentially dire personal consequences. He had gone to Belgrade, as he doubtless had many other places, to discover the truth of what was happening, and to report it to the world. The truth mattered to him, and the telling of it mattered equally. It was a compelling trait.

He looked at her smiling back at him.

'Your dimples are cute.'

'Cute?' she had not heard that word before.

'Sweet,' he said, 'pretty.'

She turned to put some glasses away, so he would not see the colour rising in her cheeks. It was very late by now, and they were the only two people left at Taksim's bar.

'What time do you finish? Can I walk you home?'

Chapter 16

'Tell me about your husband,' said Sam 'is he still your husband?'

They were enjoying the autumn sunshine outside a cafe on the bank of the Bosphorus, sitting opposite each other at a small table, fingertips entwined, watching boats of all shapes and sizes cut across the glittering water, scattering the sunlight across the surface.

'I suppose he is, although I think I have a good case for desertion.'

'His, or yours?'

Hildegard laughed. Trust Sam to be insightful.

'Both, it would appear. We seem to have bolted in opposite directions, what does that tell you?'

'That there's a war on,' he said generously. 'How did you meet, anyway?'

'Oh, he was a friend of a friend of the people I worked for. We met at a garden party somewhere, England, or Wales, I don't remember. I do remember we got talking about trees.'

'Trees? Really?'

'Yes,' Hildegard shrugged, 'I like trees. I was admiring a specimen tree in the middle of a lawn, a willow, I think it was, and he came up and started telling me all kinds of facts about it.'

'I guess he likes trees too then?'

'He's a forester. He knows a lot about trees.'

Sam nodded, leaving her space to continue.

'Bern's much older than me. I was just nineteen when we got married, he was not far off forty. Straight away we went to live in Cyprus, he worked for the Forestry Commission there, but I didn't really like it.

'No?'

'No, I didn't know anyone, and all the other ex-pat wives were older, they all had children and I found them quite a difficult group to get to know. It was different for Bern, he was busy working, he had lots of colleagues that he knew well and he was used to that life. He'd been in Cyprus for a long time, and he grew up as a Brit abroad too.'

'In Cyprus?'

'No, Burma, actually. Mandalay. His father was in the army. Scot's Guards, I think. Odd, considering he was an Irishman. Anyway, he had his family there with him, including Bern.'

'Ah, so he's a colonial brat.'

'Now you mention it. I remember his sister telling me that he had them all running rings around him. Two older sisters, two younger sisters and the entire household staff, all dancing in attendance. He was the only boy, it sounded like he ruled the roost. She said he got the most monumental shock when he was shipped off from Rangoon to boarding school in rainy Dorset at the age of twelve.'

Sam laughed.

'I'm sorry, I don't mean to offend you.'

'Not at all, I hardly feel disloyal to him, not after all this time.'

'Were you in Cyprus for long?'

'No, only a few months. I was missing home and Bern hadn't even met my family, so he took an extended leave and we went off to travel around Europe a bit, and end up in Germany. At least, that was the plan. Our daughter was born in Germany, and six months after that, he left.'

Sam raised his eyebrows.

'No wonder you don't feel disloyal talking about him.'

'That was the spring of 1939, and the British Foreign Office advice was for us all to return from Germany. Bern was supposed to find a house and a job in England, so we could join him. But he didn't, and then the war started, and then we couldn't.'

Hildegard could think of nothing more to say about Bern. It struck her how different Sam was to him, how easy to he was talk to, how interested he was in what she had to say. Bern had always been preoccupied with his work, and always seemed keener to spend time with his colleagues than with her.

'So how old's your little girl now, four?' Sam was watching her carefully, aware that this conversation could upset her. But Hildegard wanted to talk about Eleanor, she wanted to tell Sam about her.

'She'll be five next month.' Hildegard looked far across the Bosphorus waiting for the sudden tears that welled to seep back behind her eyes. She smiled wistfully.

'She's called Eleanor, after your marvelous Mrs Roosevelt. I liked the idea that she be named for such a paragon of social justice. It's like a talisman, an antidote to the swastika stamped on her birth certificate. Except the idiot registrar put a German 'e' on the end, so it says "Eleanore", but she is Eleanor."

'Do you have a photograph?'

'No. I brought some, of course, but they took them away from me at the Reich border when they were inspecting papers. I don't know why. They said I'd get them back when I returned, but I won't be going back, not until the war is over and anyway, it's my daughter I'd be going back for, not a stupid photograph.'

'She's still in Germany, then?'

'Yes, I managed to get her evacuated to the mountains, with my mother. Safe, I hope, both of them.'

More coffee arrived, and they sat in comfortable silence for a while.

'What about you? Have you never married?'

'No, Ma'am, never in one place long enough, the newspaper keeps me on my toes. I guess you would say I'm married to the job.'

They stayed a while longer, and then ambled arm in arm back up the hill. Sam left her at her apartment building and went home to type a submission for the Tribune, a report on the renewed fighting in the Aegean islands. Hildegard let herself in and found a note in her pigeonhole in the lobby. Her heart fluttered when she read that her new passport was ready, and could she kindly collect it from the British Consulate. She went straight there and was handed a manilla envelope containing the precious document, and something else. Another envelope, with a note inside indicating an appointment, expressing trust that she remember the given address and then return the note to the clerk.

Chapter 17

It was very late when she finished work, but the appointment time had taken account of her hours. She had found the address the day before, it was a narrow residential street like many others, an eclectic mix of old stone and wooden houses, comfortably nestled together in a haphazard row. It was a place where ordinary people went about their daily lives, a place scented with cooking smells and clean washing, the mothers indiscriminately and collectively responsible for the children swarming in and out of open doors. A neighbourly place, by day. In the dark, it felt prohibited, as though each house were protecting secrets with its closed shutters. The blackout was observed in Istanbul, just in case, and Hildegard was alert to every gliding shadow, every sound disowned by the darkness.

She used the white painted tree trunks and curb stones to navigate in the moonlight, her pulse pounding in her ears. Holding her coat collar closed at her throat against the cold, she walked briskly along the middle of the road until the building before her destination, then she made for the pavement. The house was unlit and she was suddenly uncertain that she had the right time and place, but as she approached, the door opened and she was courteously but swiftly drawn inside. The door closed quietly behind her.

'Good evening, Miss. This way please.'

She followed the man past the foot of the stairs and into a low lit, cosy, woodsmoke scented parlour at the back of the house.

'Sir,' said the man, standing aside to allow Hildegard forward. A second man stood to greet her.

'Mrs Reilly, a pleasure to meet you. Mac will take your coat. Please, have a seat.'

'Thank you.'

'Thank you, Mac.'

Mac retreated discreetly.

The man in the parlour was tall and slender, and moved with graceful energy. Settling again into his wing chair by the little fireplace, he rested his elbows on the arms and strummed his fingertips together, head tilted, watching her with interest through his thick rimmed round spectacles. He's not much older than me, she thought, although he looks like an eager schoolboy.

'Let's get straight to business,' he said pleasantly, 'why don't you tell me about yourself?'

'Well, I arrived here a few weeks ago,' Hildegard began tentatively.

'I mean, tell me all about yourself. Everything. Right from the beginning.' He smiled encouragingly.

It was important that this meeting went well. This was her one chance to show her good faith and she wanted more than anything to prove her sincerity. She told him about her family, her childhood and her convent education which, between Catholic conservatism and the Nazi's lack of interest in intellectual development, had been reduced to little more than training for a life of polite society and domesticity.

'And then my mother packed me off to finishing school in Prague. She despaired of me because I never really liked to do the things young ladies are supposed to do, like play the piano and do embroidery, that sort of thing. I think she thought it was her last chance to set me straight.'

He laughed, 'And did it?' he asked. Hildegard considered this for a moment.

'Yes. But not in the way she intended.'

'Tell me about the finishing school,' he had a sense that it had been a defining experience for Hildegard, and he was right.

'The finishing school was exactly that, the end of my schooldays. I went there feeling like an exiled convict, in hostile protest against my mother's insistence that I go. To me, it was just another convent school and at seventeen I had had enough of those. But actually it was very different to what I had experienced before.'

'How so?'

'It opened my eyes to what was really going on in Germany. The head of the school was a retired bishop from Canada, and he agreed to help me with my languages, French and English. They were about the only useful things I had learned at school and I wanted to improve. Especially English. So we would have lengthy conversations about all kinds of things.'

'Like what?'

'Well, the arts. He liked modern music, Gershwin in particular, and now the "Rhapsody in Blue" is a favourite of mine too. Then things he thought I should know, like discerning a fine brandy, and how to smoke cigarettes in company,' she illustrated her point by taking her little amber cigarette holder from her bag and inserting a cigarette. The man declined one but leant forward to light Hildegard's for her.

'Thank you. You see, apparently the fashionable ladies of society inhale the smoke only to their throat, and then exhale with great control and a care for where the smoke goes. How on earth he knew such things, I've no idea, but I took it all in, all these things my mother never told me.' She smiled and exhaled smoke toward the floor. 'The best thing was his arranging for me to learn to drive a coach and four and sometimes even six horses.'

'How very exciting,' he said.

'Yes, sublimely. He became like a favourite uncle to me really.' Hildegard mused. 'And we talked about politics. A lot.'

'What were those conversations like?' he asked.

She drew on her cigarette again while she found the right word. 'Revelatory.'

'Tea, Sir?' Mac had reappeared in the doorway.

'Oh, I think we can do better than that, don't you?' he said genially.

Chapter 18

Mac returned a minute later with a brass tray holding two brandy glasses and a decanter, which he set on a small coffee table and then disappeared once more. The man glanced at Hildegard as he poured their drinks.

'Go on,' he said.

'I'd always thought that I just didn't understand politics. My parents, well, my mother really, my father was always at work, I don't know what he thought, but my mother seemed to support things the government did, like providing housing for people. She never told me that the houses had been made available by forcibly removing their Jewish inhabitants and shipping them off to goodness knew where. I never heard her voice any criticism of the government.'

'So, is your mother a Nazi? Is she a member of the party?' Even so blunt a question sounded urbane coming from him.

'No. She's not a Nazi. The Nazis are evil, and she isn't that. But she doesn't think, either. Much less act. She just follows popular opinion, like every other German housewife. I don't think she gave it any more than superficial consideration. And I'd never really questioned her about it either. But when the bishop pointed out to me the rest of the story, the unfairness of the Nuremberg Laws, for example, that had just been passed, it made me think, and I did begin to understand. It dawned on me that it wasn't me that was stupid about politics, just that these particular politics did not make sense. I came to my own conclusion, that I fundamentally disagreed with the state, with the law, and with my own mother.'

'I suppose you had to go home eventually, though. What happened then?'

#

It was late winter when Hildegard left the finishing school and the day after she got home she went for a walk. It was cold still, but sunny and she was keen to reacquaint herself with the town she had been away from for six months. She walked along the canal path and around the rosengarten, stopping to watch a robin peck at the last of the red hips that capped the spikes of skeleton hedges. On her way home, she saw a school friend she had written to a couple of times while she was away, but who had not replied. She called out to her. Hildegard thought her friend must have heard her but the girl carried on walking, her head bowed as she approached a little footbridge over the canal. Hildegard ran to catch up with her.

'Liese, it's me, Hildegard! Are you alright?'

Liese stood still, staring at the ground, avoiding Hildegard's inquisitive eyes.

'Liese! I wrote to you, and you didn't write back. Are you alright?' she asked again, reaching her hand to her friend's arm. Liese shrugged her off.

'Hildegard, you mustn't speak to me,' she replied in an anxious whisper.

'What? Why not?'

'It's dangerous. Too dangerous for you and your family, and for me too.'

Before Hildegard could say anything more, Liese turned and hurried away over the bridge. She did not look back.

Anna was arranging daffodils in a vase on the kitchen table. The room was clean and tidy, serenely accepting the thin winter sun streaming in through the tall windows. She cast a critical eye over her handiwork and touched her hair to make sure no strands strayed from the tortoiseshell and seed pearl comb securing it. Satisfied on both counts, she began to clear up the superfluous flower stalks when Hildegard burst in breathlessly. The calm atmosphere shattered like glass, falling in shards to the floor.

'Mother! Mother I've just seen Liese, and she wouldn't speak to me, and she said it was dangerous and she ran away and...'

'Hildegard,' said Anna sharply, 'Compose yourself. That school was supposed to turn you into a young lady, not a wild animal.'

Hildegard took a deep breath and struggled to control herself. She knew her mother would not listen unless she could speak calmly. Anna spoke first.

'She's right, you should stay away from her, it is dangerous. For everyone.'

'But why?' wailed Hildegard, 'She's my friend, I've known her practically all my life.'

'But now we know we must only associate with other Germans, Hildegard, it is the law,' Anna explained patiently.

Hildegard stared at Anna. What was she talking about?

'But Liese is German. She's as German as I am.'

Anna looked at her daughter sternly.

'No, Hildegard. She is a Jew.'

Anna's words struck Hildegard like a slap, shocking her. It was true, the pragmatic nuns at the convent school would educate any girl as long as her family had the funds to pay the fees. The only distinction had been made for religious studies, when an amenable Rabbi visited to instruct the Jewish girls while the Catholics remained with the sisters.

#

'I was horrified at her. These people were our friends and neighbours. How could she be so cold towards them?'

'So did you have it out with her? Was there an argument between you?'

'There was a void between us. A chasm, a thousand miles wide. I didn't know how to reach her. I don't think I even wanted to.' After a moment, she continued. 'All my life, I used to climb out of my bedroom window onto the roof, and sit there thinking about things, you know. But even that didn't help that day. We barely spoke to each other after that. Apart from her trying to persuade me to join the "Faith and Beauty" lot, for young ladies such as myself, that is.'

'And did you?"

'I did not. I got myself a job and went to live in Britain.'

He smiled at that and topped up their drinks. She told him about Bern, and about Eleanor, and Bern's having to leave them. There she paused.

'I suppose once the war began, things must have been quite difficult for you, as a Brit in Germany?'

She swirled the caramel liquid around the base of the balloon glass. He now knew her intellectual position against the Nazis, and how her mind had been made up. But she needed him to understand her strength, and that meant she must trust him with her vulnerability. She took a deep breath and looked directly at him.

'When the war was declared, I was arrested immediately.'

He listened attentively, without interrupting, as she spelled out to him the horrors she had suffered, and their appalling consequences. At times, there was a tremor in her voice, but she did not falter and she did not lower her eyes. The shame was not hers.

'I was afraid of them for a very long time.'

'Of course,' he said. Then, after a moment, 'And you're not afraid now?'

'No,' she said simply. 'Somewhere along the line I stopped being afraid, stopped believing I was trapped and helpless. I began to hate them instead, but hate is such a bitter emotion, I realised I needed to act, to do something to vent it, or it would destroy me. And anyway, they are haters, the Nazis, they hate everyone who is not like them, everyone who is other. I am not like them. I don't want to be like them.'

'What, then?' he asked, 'What do you want? Revenge?'

Hildegard shook her head.

'Justice,' she said, quietly. 'I want justice. And for that to happen, first they must be defeated'

A muscle twitched in her jaw.

Sir nodded his understanding.

'I see.' They shared a contemplative silence, which he eventually broke with a conversational, 'Actually, I've already made some enquiries since you appeared at the Consulate,' he poured her more brandy 'and your story checked out, I'm glad to say. I think you could be quite useful. I'm pleased to hear that you are still of a mind to help.'

Hildegard brightened.

'Oh, absolutely, Mr.?'

'Splendid. Splendid,' he said, ignoring her question. 'Let's get started, then. No time like the present. As I recall, our friend Wolff at the German Consulate is expecting you to deliver to him what morsels of information you can, is that right?'

'Yes, although I haven't been to see him yet, not since the day I arrived.'

'No, I know. That's alright, you have only been here a few weeks, but now that you have settled in, met a few people, I'm sure he will send you a summons soon.'

How did he know that she hadn't been to see Wolff? How did he know she had been told not to initiate the next contact? He continued,

'This is what we will do. I'm going to give you things to tell him, some of it will be true, and some of it misleading. Chickenfeed, we call it. We want him to trust you, so he needs to be able to verify what you are telling him, especially at the start, but once he does trust you, then we can lead him wherever we like.'

Hildegard nodded.

'Alright. I hope I can be convincing.'

'You won't know which of it is true and which not. That will make it easier for you to deliver consistently, and don't forget, as far as he is concerned it is just hearsay anyway, things you've picked up from customers at work. He will take it seriously, but he won't blame you if it turns out to be wrong.'

'Alright.'

'We scatter our chickenfeed quite generously. The idea is that if they hear the same thing from several sources, they are more likely to give it credence, do you see?'

'Yes, the more people there are saying something, the more likely it is to be true.'

'Exactly. Of course, if he were to let slip any information in return…'

'Of course.'

He sat back in his chair, looking at her for a moment, with a grave expression.

'There is one more thing, that it is my duty to inform you. If anything happens to you, we know nothing about you. Is that understood?'

A minute ago, Hildegard had been excited by the thought of doing her bit, however small, she was proud of joining the Allied war effort. But the support they offered in return was quicksand. They would not help her if she were caught. If she found herself in trouble, she would be on her own.

'Understood,' she said without hesitation. 'What shall I tell him first?'

Chapter 19

'Good morning, Sir,' the clerk called as he passed through the lobby.

That morning he had kissed his darling wife goodbye and made the short journey from his apartment, energetically on foot as usual, to Pera House. He headed up the grand marble staircase beneath the grand chandelier and nodded to His Majesty as he passed below his portrait. He carried on apace up the narrow back stairs to his office on the top floor, reciprocating the cheery greetings of the eclectic but remarkably affable collection of people that were his colleagues at the British Consulate as he went. To a man, they would describe themselves as typical office workers, passport clerks, archivists and the like. Every last one of them, just like himself, was tasked with some secret trickery or other. He liked them, they were an interesting bunch, but then, most people were, in his opinion.

Despite the late night, he had made an early start because his next report to the Cairo headquarters of SIME, Security and Intelligence Middle East, was due and he wanted to include his latest news. Every couple of weeks he, and all his counterparts across the Middle East, submitted a summary of events and people in their patch. The collated Security Summary Middle East report, designated Most Secret, was then disseminated back to them from Cairo HQ so each district representative was kept up to date across the region.

The reports sometimes read like a telephone directory, lists of lost passports were a regular feature, but usually there were some informative pieces that were more entertaining. The Middle East was swarming with colourful characters, each ploughing their own furrow in the global battlefield. This time, he had several comings and goings to report from Istanbul. There were a handful of Arabian refugees who wanted to lose themselves in the Turkish interior rather than be deported back home; an Austrian quisling Government minister who had apparently had an epiphany and was looking for friends among the Allies who would help him re-establish an independent Austria; an assortment of Nazi sympathisers; a Syrian businessman with a lucrative sideline in gold smuggling, and Hildegard.

What to say about Hildegard? he pondered. She had arrived out of the blue all those weeks ago, like a gift almost too good to be true. Naturally, he had been sceptical when her improbable story was first relayed to him. But he had diligently made enquiries all the same. The errant husband was fairly easily located in the West Country, and had, by all accounts, very readily swapped his tale of woe for a pint of beer. His poor young wife and child, left to the mercy of Hitler and he, tragically, unable to rescue them.
Pathetic really, but at least he had unwittingly confirmed her story. The young wife, on the other hand, had shown herself to have rather more gumption in extricating herself from the predicament he had left her in. Her inventive story about her sap of a husband being related to the British Ambassador at Ankara had amused him. He could just imagine Sir Hughe raising an eyebrow at that. It would not, of course, be in his report for HQ, but he would save it up as an anecdote for his chums at White's, his London club, when the war was over.

Hildegard had given a good account of herself at their first meeting last night. There was nothing in the retelling of her story that had given him cause for concern, no gaps or inconsistencies. If she had made it all up, something would have slipped, but nothing had. It was plausible that she was genuine, and his intuition told him that she was. But still, he would wait and see. After all, she had not yet been tested.

He decided that he would report that she was more recently arrived than she actually was, to avoid awkward questions about why he had not reported on her sooner, and he would be brief in his description. It was good practice that his secret agents were his secret alone, safer for them, safer for him. If she proved unreliable, he could always drop her, denounce her if necessary, at some later date. He had set her a good test, her first step toward gaining Wolff's confidence. She had seemed a little surprised by it, which was only natural, but she had willingly agreed to carry out his instructions. He hoped that she would prove useful, and her first task would certainly test her resolve, but only time would tell for certain. For now, he wrote:

Hildegard Reilly (nee Brabender), German widow of a former English official in Cyprus, arrived in Istanbul from Bucharest on 21 October 43, travelling on a German passport. An unconfirmed report states that she has been sent to Istanbul on a mission by the Germans.

It was a conservative summary that was all more or less true, apart from the date of her arrival, and the judicious killing off of her husband. There was no need for anyone to go looking for him now. All that was left was to see what happened next.

Chapter 20

Silesia, Winter 1943-1944

Winter came early to the mountains and the little village of Kiesewald was snowed in weeks before Christmas. This brought some difficulties in that the only way to stock up on provisions was to sledge down the slope to the next village, which was larger and had a better supply of essentials. Once the sledges were loaded with necessities, they were strung together in a train and hauled back up the mountain by an elderly horse with incongruous jingling bells on its harness. Erika and Hedda had to walk back with the other older children because the horse was not strong enough to pull them as well as the laden sledges up the hill, but they did so with their usual good humour, laughing and throwing snowballs at each other as they went.
Eleanor was allowed to go with them, wrapped in every woollen item of clothing Anna could find, and a blanket for good measure. Because she was so small, she was perched atop the load on a sledge with the blanket tucked around her and had a ride back up the mountain too. The girls grumbled good-

naturedly all the way back and teased her about being a princess, but Eleanor didn't mind, she felt special being the only one not having to walk.

One crisp cold mountain day followed another and the daylight seemed increasingly rationed like everything else. Christmas came and went, marked only by carols and a general feeling of goodwill among the neighbours. Eleanor received a picture book from one of the many cousins. She was not quite certain who had sent the book, but she loved it and was glad they had. It was about the adventures of a little girl called Klarchen, who was always in some sort of trouble. Eleanor thought Klarchen was very funny, but she would never dare to be so naughty herself.

Weeks passed and winter had a firm frozen grip on the mountain, with no respite in sight, when a plain brown postcard arrived from Anna's youngest brother, Herman.

> 'Viel Liebe und kuss
> von euer Herman
> der soldat sein muss'

Much love and a kiss, he wrote, from your Herman, who has to be a soldier. He had been drafted into the army and shipped off to the eastern front to freeze in the mud and snow. The Wehrmacht and the Red Army remained static, glaring at each other across the icy battlefields, but Herman had been granted some leave and was coming to visit.
Eleanor did not remember her uncle, she had not seen him since she was a baby. He was actually, of course, her great-uncle, but being so much younger than Anna, he was closer in age to Hildegard. Everyone in the house was excited about having a visitor.

As the train puffed away from the platform Uncle Herman slung his pack on the sledge and trudged up the hill beside the horse. He was a quiet young man, made quieter still by his profound war weariness, and he was a little overwhelmed by the household's enthusiastic welcome. After the best meal they could muster, for which Herman was sincerely thankful, he excused himself and went to bed.

He slept until late the following morning and came down to find the kitchen a quiet haven, occupied only by his sister and niece. Anna placed a breakfast plate before him on the table.

'You look a little better this morning, did you sleep well?'

'I did, thank you. Nothing better for that than mountain air, is there?'

Anna sat down opposite him. She was the second eldest of their family, having one older sister. Between her and Herman had been six other siblings, and all but one of the boys had survived infancy. Herman had always been her favourite though, perhaps because he was one of the youngest. She had been old enough to help when he was a baby, and she had become like a second mother to him.

'Herman,' she began, 'You took a risk, writing that card.'

'What do you mean?' said Herman with his mouth full. He was not defensive, he had just forgotten what he wrote.

'"Who has to be a soldier". What a thing to say! I've heard they shoot people for less, you know, you should be more careful. Show you are loyal.'

Herman looked at his sister thoughtfully.

'I am loyal to every man that has the misfortunate to be out there, just like me,' he said. 'I am loyal, to my friends. Anyway, the top brass won't shoot me,' he finished quietly.

'How do you know that? Are you so special? They might.'

Anna had had every intention to chide her brother gently, but she felt her fear for him rising into panic.

'They won't.' Herman said patiently, he knew how she worried and he wanted to reassure her. They might have been far apart in age, but of all their siblings, she was the one he felt closest to, the one he loved the most.

'I'm not special,' he explained, 'but I am a mechanic, and that's as good. I am the only man in my company who can keep our Major's car running in that godforsaken wasteland. Even the panzers struggled, I've never seen snow and ice and mud like it.' He would say no more about the front. Anna had no idea what it was like out there, and that was neither her fault, nor something he wished to rectify. She did not need to know, and it was better for her that she didn't, it would only fuel her worry for him. She squeezed his hands resting on the table, accepting his explanation and making a connection, a peace offering.

'Just be careful,' she said quietly.

'So, Eleanor, you are quite the big girl now, aren't you? How old are you? Three? Four?' Herman turned to his niece.

'I'm five!' said Eleanor, indignation winning over shyness.

'Five!' said Herman, 'that's definitely old enough to know your way around. How about showing me where everything is here?' Eleanor nodded, delighted at this honour and once bundled into hat, coat, scarf, mitts and boots, took Herman's hand and showed him the yard and where the goats lived. They went into the snowy lane and walked down to the end of the village. At the edge of the forest, Hermann kicked around among the gravelly stones beneath the trees and picked up some small pieces of wood, examining them carefully, placing some in his pockets and discarding others.

'Is that for kindling?' asked Eleanor, wondering why he took such care over choosing it.

'No, not kindling,' said Herman.

'What's it for, then?' asked Eleanor after a few seconds consideration.

She could not work it out. Herman winked at her.

'Wait and see,' he said.

When they returned to the kitchen, he placed the wood near the stove and told Anna not to put it in the fire. She nodded, she seemed to know what is was for, but Eleanor was still mystified.

The next morning, when Eleanor came into the kitchen, she noticed immediately that the pieces of wood had gone. Herman saw her looking for them and reached into his shirt pocket.

'Are you looking for this?' he said with a smile. Eleanor's eyes widened and she stared up at him, and then down again at the perfect wooden cat, curled up asleep in his hand. She gasped, amazed at it.

'It's for you, a gift,' he said, 'I hope you like it?'

Eleanor took it reverently. It had fit comfortably on Herman's palm, but she needed both of her small hands to hold it. She placed the cat carefully on the table and stroked its smooth round back, following the grain of the wood, just like the nap of real fur, with her finger, looking at it in wonderment. Now she had three precious things of her very own, her doll, her Klarchen book and Uncle Herman's cat. The beautiful cat was the most special of all because Uncle Herman had whittled it himself, just for her.

'Thank you, Uncle Herman,' she said, looking up at him, 'I like it very much.'

Over the following days, Eleanor sat with Herman, watching entranced as he whittled more creatures from the pieces of wood. He showed her how to look at each one, how to turn it over and allow her fingers to follow its lines and curves, to feel as much as see what it wanted to be. The cat was obvious from the curve of the grain, and here a pointed snout, a fox, or a dog perhaps, what did she think? What about this gnarly piece? It looks cross like it doesn't want to be anything other than a lump of wood.

'A goat then,' said Eleanor, 'they're the grumpiest creatures of all!'

The goat was less successful than the other animals, Herman said the wood would not cooperate, and that proved that Eleanor was right. By the end of his leave, she had seen him liberate the forms of a menagerie of creatures from shapeless beginnings. Eleanor's cat was her favourite, she put it on the windowsill in her and Anna's room beneath the steep eaves, where it could sleep in the sun, undisturbed. The rest she placed thoughtfully around the house, a dog to guard the kitchen door, a turtle by the sink and the miserable goat in the yard with the others.

Herman would always choose to be outside, and avoided being 'cooped up', as he called it, at all costs. Eleanor wanted to spend her days with Herman.

'She'll catch her death,' warned Anna, whose natural habitat had walls and a roof. 'You know she has a weak chest, don't you?'

'Well then, the fresh air will do her good. Come on Eleanor, let's wrap you up, those snowballs won't throw themselves.'

Eleanor giggled, she had never heard anyone win an argument over Grandma before. In lieu of having the last word, Anna made a show of firmly retying Eleanor's scarf but she smiled an unseen, indulgent smile at their backs as they ventured out.

That day repeated itself, again and again, in a perfect little cycle of contentment. Often it was getting dark when the adventurers reappeared, Herman trudging slowly back up the slope with an exhausted, rosy cheeked Eleanor on his shoulders. He was careful though, that they were never late for the evening meal.

One night, as he was tucking her into bed, Eleanor asked sleepily

'Uncle Herman, shall we go and look for wood tomorrow? I think we need some more animals.' Herman smoothed the little girl's hair and sighed.

'There is nothing I would like to do more, Eleanor, but I'm sorry, we can't. I have to go back tomorrow.'

'Back where?' Eleanor was suddenly wide awake and sitting up.

'To the army.'

'When will you come here again?'

'I don't know. But I promise I will do my very best to come back as soon as I can. It might not be for a long time, though. Alright?' Eleanor nodded sadly and threw her arms around Herman's waist.

'Will you promise me something too?' She nodded again, not letting go.

'I want you to look after all the wooden animals, can you do that?'

She loosened her grip a little and looked up at him.

'I wish you could stay, Uncle Herman.' Her small voice and damp cheeks were almost unbearable to him. He turned off the light and sat with her in the dark, stroking the back of her hand with his thumb, until eventually she slept. He took a picture postcard from his shirt pocket and left it on her bedside table. It was a watercolour picture of a small child asleep in a cot, surrounded by angels.

'Fourteen angels to watch over you, little one,' he whispered.

Herman left before the sun rose the following day, his backpack nudging him on with each bounding stride down the hill toward the station. He was to re-join his platoon as it journeyed west.

Eleanor did not smile and hardly spoke during the next few days, but she took her promise to Herman very seriously. She wandered around the house, checking the animal hiding places, moving some into pairs if she thought they looked lonely, making sure never to group two that might fight, she even moved the goat across the yard to give it a different view.

'Maybe this will cheer you up,' she told it.

'Eleanor's not herself since Herman left,' Maria said to Anna as she tidied the kitchen one evening. Anna put down her darning with a sigh.

'No, I know. Poor little thing. First her father abandons them, then her mother goes off on her own odyssey and now Herman has gone too. She's been left behind by every adult in her life, it seems.'

Maria turned to look at her friend.

'Well, you know, she still has you.'

'Yes,' said Anna, 'she will always have me.'

Chapter 21

Istanbul, February 1944

The haunting early call to prayer often drifted on the prevailing wind, through her open window and into Hildegard's sleep. Sometimes, it wove itself into the fabric of her dream, neither invited nor acknowledged, gently bestowing its ethereal presence. Sometimes, it roused her and she woke with a feeling of peace. One morning, a few weeks into the new year, Hildegard was jolted awake before this gentle intrusion by the hoarse ring of the doorbell of her apartment. Struggling to open her eyes after a very late night, she focussed sufficiently on the clock to see that it was too early for visitors. She closed her eyes again, but the ringing persisted. There it was again. She rose reluctantly, pulling her brush through her hair as she passed the dresser and her robe about her as she went to answer the door. Whoever it was had rung a third time, it must be important. It had better be.

There was nobody there. Somebody playing a prank, no doubt. Hildegard was not amused. As she stepped back to close the door, a shallow basket slid into sight along the landing floor, with a ball of white angora wool in it. She peered at it, but her mind was still vague with sleep and she could not understand what it was, nor why it was there. Curious, she leant down for a closer look, and heard a cough from Sam, who was leaning against the wall at the top of the stairs.

'Morning. Can we come in?'

'It's the middle of the night,' Hildegard said, with a sigh, 'And who is "we"?'

'It's seven o'clock. Me, and him,' said Sam, indicating the basket.

Hildegard looked again at the ball, which partially uncurled itself and looked back at her with round black eyes. They blinked at each other.

'What is it?' she said.

'It's a he, and he's a puppy. A fine Pomeranian. A prince from the islands in the Sea of Marmara, the very finest of his breed.' said Sam, as he deftly picked up the basket and closed the door behind himself.

'You'd better come in then,' muttered Hildegard, following him back along the corridor to the living room. 'Why have you brought it here?'

'I need somewhere for him to stay. Just a few hours. I have a really important piece to write, some Germans from the Consulate here have defected, it's got to be wired in today. I'll come and get him at lunchtime. Please?'

'Does it have a name?' Ignoring the news of the defections, Hildegard looked dubiously first at the puppy, and then at his deliverer.

'Not yet, he's just a baby. Why don't you think of something to call him?'

Hildegard thought Sam would not much like what she wanted to call the puppy at that moment, nor him for that matter, so she said nothing.

'Can he stay?' Sam and the puppy both stared at her with the same pleading expression. Hildegard sighed.

'Make yourself a coffee and close the door behind you when you leave. I'm going back to bed.'

'So can he stay?'

'I suppose so.' Hildegard said reluctantly as she wandered back along the corridor to her room. By the time she had hung up her robe, the puppy was already turning circles on the mat.

Predictably, Sam did not return until late in the afternoon. Hildegard had slept again until just before lunchtime, curled up around her little house guest who had somehow contrived to be allowed on the bed. She had to admit he was rather sweet, a white fluffy body with velvet triangle ears, a black nose and those deep black eyes, infinite as the universe. Her irritation at the rude early awakening faded as she and the puppy became acquainted.
She walked up the road to a restaurant owned by some friendly Hungarians who happily gave her a bone for the puppy to chew. When he tired of that, she played with him until he needed to sleep again, grudgingly admitting to herself that he was nice to have around. When Sam eventually did reappear, Hildegard was prepared to agree for the puppy to stay for a few days.

The next day, Hildegard went to the veterinary surgery and bought some flea powder. The puppy might be welcome, but his passengers were not. The flea powder was grey and had to be liberally applied and then left on for several hours before washing it off, during which time the puppy looked rather forlorn.
'He looks like a rat,' said Sam bluntly.
'Oh, no!' Hildegard was surprised at how protective of the little creature she felt. 'Not a rat. A mouse, perhaps,' she conceded.
So the puppy found his name. He was Mouse.

Weeks passed and Hildegard and Sam watched Mouse grow into a fine, handsome dog. He was intelligent and knew his own mind, which was often turned to mischief. He soon developed an endearing habit of following Hildegard to the door when she went out, and lying on the floor there, waiting for her to return. More than once though, his sense of adventure got the better of him, and when he saw the opportunity as the door opened, he absconded at pace from the apartment. Hildegard would race after him, her irritation at his willfulness outweighed by her admiration for his unfailing ability to spot and evade the scorpions that lurked in the storm drains. She avoided them too, following the same line Mouse took on his helter-skelter escape to the Bosphorus shore.

Aside from trying, and failing, to train Mouse, Hildegard's time was filled with work. She spent the evenings at Taksim's, with occasional after hours visits to Sir in the back room of the little house where she had first met him. During the day, she began teaching English again. It was something she had enjoyed in Berlin, despite the circumstances, but her students here were far more diverse and interesting. One of them was a Hungarian called Peter. He was a couple of years younger than Hildegard and had left Budapest to study history and politics in Istanbul just before the war began. She sometimes despaired of him ever speaking intelligible English, often having no idea if he had the right word because his accent was so strong his pronunciation was awful. But she could not fault his perseverance, nor his sense of humour, and they became friends.

After busy working weeks, Hildegard looked forward to the weekends. Sam would visit his favourite haunts on Saturday nights, meeting friends in Ellie's Bar or the Snake Pit, or sometimes venturing up the coast to the Tokatlian Hotel, but by closing time he was at the end of the bar in Taksim's Casino, waiting to walk home with her. They lazed in bed on Sunday mornings until as late as Mouse would allow before he crawled his way up the bed between them, demanding a walk.

'What made you want to be a journalist?' Hildegard asked as they wandered slowly to a café for breakfast one weekend.

'My dad first,' said Sam, 'he was a newspaper man. And then my school.'

'Did your dad travel much, like you?'

'Not really, he worked for a local paper where we lived, in New York state. But he always had an interesting story to tell, I used to love to listen to him. Everyone has their own unique story, he used to say. Then, at Yale, I realised that often those stories were versions of the same event, just told from different perspectives.'

'How do you know which to believe? When you're hearing different versions of the same events, how do you know which version is the truth?' asked Hildegard.

'They all are, to a certain degree. That's what's fascinating to me, you listen to different people's versions of a story, you get to know their points of view, and some opinions you agree with and some you don't, but they all help you learn and understand the whole story.'

'It's not easy to listen to someone whose opinion is repugnant to you,' said Hildegard.

'No, but if you listen respectfully to all sides, then you can write what is hopefully a balanced and objective commentary. And that is your truth.'

Hildegard sat in the early spring sunshine outside the café. She watched Sam throw a ball for Mouse and felt a wave of affection for them both. Mouse was now a striking creature, his sturdy body, with its thick white coat contrasting his black nose and eyes, stood proud on strong legs, his feathery tail curled over his back, ready to run after the ball. Sam's presumption that he was the best of his breed had proven true and earned him a promotion to a title. Mouse had grown up, now he was Mr. Mouse, her beloved companion.

She wondered how Sam had known, better than she had known herself, how much she had needed Mouse. He had realised that having Mouse for company, caring for him, would go some way to distracting her from the pain of her separation from Eleanor. Not only was he an astute observer of human nature, of her nature, but he had had the sensitivity to act with such kindness to help her.

When she first arrived in Istanbul, Hildegard had not known a soul and at times felt lonely and scared. But she was there with a sense of purpose and that gave her strength, the courage of her convictions, Schuddekopf would have said. Since then, she had built a life here, even began to feel settled. As well as Mouse now, she had her job at Taksim's, her work for Sir, her teaching, her apartment, her friends, Sam. A full life. She was content. Happy, even. But that cast a shadow, and the only person who could begin to understand was Peter.

He had left his family behind in Nazi territory, still at risk from the war, still living on rations, still without him there to help them, just as Hildegard's were without her. He understood some of the worry and the guilt of having left people he loved behind in such circumstances, and he sympathised with Hildegard.

She knew that their situations were different though, and she could not share the worst of her guilt, even with him. He had been a boy when he left, sent away by his family with the best intentions so that he could study in safety. Hildegard had made decisions for her family that she had no way of knowing would be right for them. Would they really be safer in the south? She questioned her own motivations again and again. Had she been selfish? She kept telling herself that she had done the best she could in trying times. Of all of her family, she had been the one to suffer the most under the Nazi's and no-one would begrudge her escaping that. And she was still in danger here too, Sir repeatedly made that clear. But the difference was that here, she was free. Free of the worst of the Nazi oppression, free to live as she pleased, free of the responsibility of being Eleanor's mother.

Chapter 22

'Afternoon post for you, Sir.'

He slid the largest manilla envelope from the bottom of the pile, already knowing what it contained. Security Summary Middle East No.176, the usual midweek missive from his Cairo headquarters, this one dated Wednesday 5th April 1944. Preceding the first item was a pointed reminder not to share the content with anybody not on the distribution list unless absolutely necessary, and then with a clear caveat about the need for secrecy. Interesting. There must have been a breach somewhere. He scanned the reports from his colleagues scattered across the region.

King Farouk appears to have been on a successful popularity crusade in Egypt. Good for him. Reading between the lines from Cairo, there seemed to be a surge of political interest among the population in general, including some student unease at the American attitude to Jewish immigration into Palestine. That may prove problematic, he mused.

From Palestine itself, it seemed the British mandate to be an equitable broker between Arab and Jew was looking less and less feasible, with the Americans supporting open entry to a Jewish homeland in Palestine, and Arabs across the region resisting. The dilemma as he saw it was that the question of a Zionist state needed concentrated global attention and so could not possibly be resolved until after this war ended, but the Jews were in dire need of help immediately, to say the least. He sighed. There was nothing he could usefully contribute to solving that particular conundrum so he drew himself back to the issues at hand.

Some civil unrest in Cyprus, which seemed to have settled itself. Similar, although more serious occurrences in Syria. A small group of expeditionary Germans and their equipment captured in Persia. Bravo. But some rancour between the nomadic tribes and the government that had the potential to escalate. Relative calm in Iraq, other than the universal rumblings about the Zionist question. And finally, item 7, his report from Turkey. A list of suspected German subversives active in the country on behalf of the Abwehr, the German military intelligence, and this:

Confirmatory evidence has been received that Mrs Hildegard Reilly, described in Security Summary No. 163 para. 6 (b) as a possible German agent who was attempting to obtain information from British and American visitors to the Casino Bar, Istanbul, is in fact in touch with the German Intelligence Service. She is known to be in contact with Bruno Wolf, Chief of Gestapo and S.D. in Istanbul and to receive substantial financial support from the German Consulate. Her address is: Chifte Vav Sokak, Esen, Apt.11/1.

That first crucial mission that he had given her last autumn had both anchored her and cut her adrift. Neither then nor since had she questioned his orders, and every time she delivered on the tasks asked of her, he felt more justified in having set her on this path, and more disquieted by it.

Chapter 23

Kiesewald, Silesia April 1944

Soon after Herman left, news came of a greater distraction, there was to be another visitor in the mountains. This time, someone Eleanor's own age was coming to stay. Anna's youngest sister Agnes, the ninth of her siblings, already had three young daughters, and had just given birth to her fourth. The eldest, Marianne, had learning difficulties due, so the family legend went, to being dropped on the floor by a nurse as a baby. Marianne had recently been admitted for care in a special children's ward. The third child Helga, still a toddler, remained with Agnes while she nursed baby Ruth, and that left Inge, who was just a few months younger than Eleanor.

Inge travelled to Silesia with another family who were being evacuated. Anna and an excited Eleanor went to the station to meet her, hurrying down the hill as they saw the long plume of smoke from the engine approaching below. After thank yous and farewells had been exchanged with Inge's travelling companions, they started the slow return journey uphill on foot. Inge was a frail child, and her lank hair and sallow complexion made her look a little wretched. She trailed a couple of steps behind them.

'Don't worry, Inge, your case will come up later on the sledge,' Eleanor turned her head, smiling. Inge looked at her dolefully and nodded. Eleanor tried again.

'Did you like it on the train?' Inge only shrugged at this, still she did not speak. Eleanor looked at Anna for help.

'I expect you're very tired, aren't you Inge? You have had such a long journey. Come along, girls, let's just get back, then we can have some lunch.' They walked the rest of the way in silence. Lunch was rescued by the lively presence of the two older girls of the house and their mother, but Anna noticed that Inge ate very little and spoke not at all.

'Do you think she likes it here?' Eleanor asked Anna, when Inge went for a nap after lunch.

'Well, she has only just arrived, give her a chance to get used to it.'

'She doesn't say anything.'

'Eleanor, she's been travelling a whole day and night, with people she doesn't know, and she doesn't really know us either, even though we are her family. So she's very tired, and probably a bit scared, and sad to be away from her mother and sisters, don't you think?'

Eleanor did think. She thought a lot about what her Grandma had said. Later, when Inge stepped tentatively into the kitchen, Eleanor went across to her and took her hand.

'Come on,' she said quietly, 'I'll show you Uncle Herman's animals.'

'Uncle Herman? My Uncle Herman?' Inge brightened a little.

'Yes, he's my uncle too.'

By the end of Herman's animal trail, they were chattering and giggling together like little girls the world over.

Some weeks later, it was Inge's birthday. By now the snow line had retreated above the meadow, revealing a green carpet bejewelled with wild flowers. The entire household carried a basket and blankets up for a birthday picnic. Inge was wearing a new dress, lovingly and expertly conjured by Anna out of one donated by Hedda, and a rather less magical flower garland in her hair, made by Eleanor with no expertise but at least as much love. The meadow was ebulliently awake after its long winter sleep. Snow melt channelled into rapid icy streams that tumbled, opaque blue-green, purling over rocks and boulders in their race to the valley. They watched a family of deer pick its way cautiously out of the woods above, and inexplicably skitter back in again.

Anna gazed at the Giant Mountains, stretching far into the distance, the white peaks stark against the bluest sky, and felt the tranquility of it all seep into her bones. Somewhere over those hills, far away, was her only daughter. She sent a silent prayer to her neglected Catholic God to keep Hildegard safe.

Maria finished laying out the picnic and settled down on the rug with Anna. They watched Inge and Eleanor playing on the slope, rolling down the hill, sending up waves of bees and butterflies before them, then walking back up, their arms linked and their heads together giggling, to do it again and again.

'It really feels like spring at last,' said Maria. 'It's lovely to watch the girls playing like that. It reminds me of when Erika and Hedda were little, not so long ago, really.'

'My daughter never played such games. I suppose, being an only child it was different for her, although she had a lot of cousins. But she always preferred her own company. She would take her dog on endless walks, and whenever I suggested she should be more sociable, she would just shrug and say she liked being on her own.'

'It's a bit of a shock when you realise your little girl has a mind of her own, isn't it?' Maria laughed sympathetically.

'It is,' Anna smiled ruefully. 'You think you are doing your best for them, doing what's right, and then you find they have other ideas entirely. It makes you question whether your best was good enough.'

'You are a good mother, Anna,' Maria squeezed her hand, 'I can see that from how you care for Eleanor and Inge. Their mothers would not have entrusted them to you if they did not agree, would they?'

God knew, Anna had tried, but Hildegard had always been a headstrong child, determinedly following her own path, compliant when it suited her, defiant when it did not. She had thought the Prague finishing school would polish her sharp edges, but she had come back from there more intent on rebellion than ever. There were sparks between them on many issues and Hildegard's new political awareness was highly inflammable. Back then, Anna had despaired of making her see that the government wanted only the best for the German people. They had, after all, housed people and given them jobs, they had been good for the nation at the start, hadn't they? Now though, all these years later, she had to concede that perhaps Hildegard had been right. She had witnessed her daughter's suffering at Nazi hands and now they were separated by a vicious war that may see Eleanor grow up without her mother. There was no good in a government based on such cruelty.

'I did my best for her,' said Anna, 'and now I do the same for them.'

'That is all any of us can do,' said Maria.

'I wonder, can a mother ever stop worrying about her children?'

They watched the little girls picking wildflowers in the meadow and smiled at each other with a melancholy empathy.

Later in the spring, the time came for Inge to go home. She was excited at the prospect of being reunited with her mother and sisters, but Eleanor was quiet in the days before she left. She was sad of course, to be losing her friend and playmate, but she was secretly a little envious too. Eleanor had no sisters, not even a brother, and it had been such a very long time since she had seen her mother.

On the station platform, while Anna was talking to Inge's chaperone for the journey, Eleanor shyly handed Inge an awkward little package, clumsily wrapped and tied with string.

'So you don't forget us,' she said.

Inge peered under the paper, then looked up, beaming. It was Herman's dog, that Eleanor knew was her favourite of the wooden animals.

Anna and Eleanor stayed on the platform, waving until the train disappeared. They would miss her, of course, but there was consolation for Eleanor in Inge's delight with her gift, and for Anna in the fact that a child who had arrived thin and wan was going home healthy and honey coloured, with roses in her cheeks.

Chapter 24

Istanbul, May 1944

Springtime was beautiful in Istanbul. There was blossom on the trees, and the sky and sea were an optimistic palette of sparkling blues. Sitting outside their favourite cafe by the Bosphorus with Sam, Mr Mouse snoozing contentedly at their feet, Hildegard watched a butterfly rest on a sun warmed stone and gently flap its damp new wings dry.

'What are you doing Sunday?' Sam asked.

'Sleeping. I'm working tomorrow evening,' Hildegard said. 'Why?'

'We, that is, me and a guest, have been invited on a boat trip. A picnic. Would you like to come?' He was smiling hopefully at her. 'Should be fun.'

'Whose boat is it?' Hildegard wondered what she was letting herself in for. Sam knew everyone in Istanbul it seemed, so this trip could be with practically anybody.

'British Consulate staff. At least, they've hired it for the day. The plan is to sail upstream and stop at some beach or other. Mr Mouse can come too. What do you say?'

Hearing his name, Mr Mouse's eyes and ears lifted. He tilted his head first at Sam and then at Hildegard.

'See, Mouse wants to go, he thinks it's a good idea.'

Hildegard laughed at them both looking expectantly at her.

'I don't suppose I've much choice, have I? It does sound nice. We'll come. Thank you, Sam.'

Another fine day dawned for the boat trip, and everybody meeting at the quay was in good spirits. There was quite a crowd of them, and it took some time to load hampers and blankets and parasols onto the boat, with Mr Mouse on his best behaviour and strictly forbidden to help. Hildegard looked at her fellow passengers. Some of them were familiar, she had seen them at Taksim's Casino, or at the British Consulate, or on evenings out in the Park Hotel or Ellie's bar, but she did not know them. They were a friendly bunch and included her cheerfully in their chatter as Sam introduced her, keeping a reassuring hand on the small of her back, knowing she was nervous about meeting his friends.

Eventually they set sail. Sam and Hildegard sat near the bow as the Turkish captain navigated his vessel expertly through the traffic near the bank and out into the wide open channel. They passed the mosques and castles and palaces along the European shore.

'It all looks so different from here,' said Hildegard, taking it all in. She knew the busy streets of the west bank and their daily routines well, but now her eyes were drawn upwards, where the towers and minarets pierced the sky and saw that they rose above the ordinary toward higher aspirations.

Quickly and inevitably, Sam's attention shifted to the water. He was a skilled sailor himself and had sailed the Bosphorus often. He showed Hildegard the flow of the water in a way she had never considered before. Where she saw only either waves or flat water, Sam understood the channel, he read the currents and the conditions, he knew how the water flowed.

'See there?' Sam said, as they sailed past Galataseray Island. He was pointing to a patch ahead where the light was dancing in squares on the water's surface. 'That means there's a gust of wind blowing sideways, it makes a ripple that cross-hatches with the current, that's why the light looks different, it has a rougher surface to reflect off. Now look, just in front of this headland, in the bay there's an eddy current, where the water swirls back in the opposite direction to the main current, like a whirlpool.'

'How did you know?' asked Hildegard.

'Because the land jutting out into the channel disturbs the flow of the water, so it curls back around on itself. Look, there.'

Hildegard followed his finger and saw the water surface change again, just as he had predicted. His obvious love of the water was infectious and Hildegard was fascinated. She rested her chin on her forearms on the rail, and watched the water with a newly educated interest, enjoying the warmth of the sun and the salt wind on her face, noticing the endless variety of patterns as the light played across what she had previously considered just water. She smiled at the jumble of prettily painted wooden houses in Bebek, packed together on the shore, jostling for the best view. Over to the east, the Anatolian bank was more sparsely populated with just a scattering of houses across the wood-covered hillsides stretching away from the water. Funny, Hildegard thought, how seeing somewhere familiar from a new perspective could make a day trip feel like a holiday. Eventually they reached the beach for the picnic and disembarked chaotically onto a tiny wooden jetty.

'So, that's your first sailing trip done. Now you're salted,' said Sam as they spread out their blanket on the sand. He planted the pole and two spokes of a large parasol in the sand, so Hildegard could sit in the shade. 'Come on, Mouse, let's go see what the water's like.'

Hildegard lay on the blanket feeling warm and grateful as she watched the two of them splashing at the water's edge. Perhaps she drifted momentarily into sleep, but voices the other side of her parasol jolted her awake. She heard Sam's name mentioned, and more, before the speaker and his companion walked past the end of her blanket, not noticing she was there.

'I'm starving, what's in the basket?' Sam laughed as he fell dripping on the blanket next to her. Hildegard leaned toward him and nodded in the direction of the man she had heard speaking, now further along the beach and out of earshot.

'Who is that man? Bill something?'

'Bill Burland? He works in the Consulate, something to do with shipping. I think he polices the Lausanne Convention. Why?'

'I don't think he likes me.'

'What makes you say that?'

'Oh, I overheard him say something. I wasn't eavesdropping, I don't think he realised I was right behind him. Or maybe he did.' She tried to sound flippant, but Sam was not fooled.

'What did he say?'

Hildegard pulled in her chin, puffed out her cheeks and blustered '"Brewer, yes, Brewer is an excellent man. One of ours, you know. I can't for the life of me think why he insists on going around with that German woman from Taksim's. I hear she is in regular contact with the German legation, and not only that, she has, ahem, gentleman callers at her flat."'

Hildegard's imitation made Sam laugh.

'It's not funny. Just because he was nice about you. I have a British passport, you know.'

'Yes, but you did come here from Germany. Look, Bill's alright. He's an accountant by profession, and you know those bean counters, they see things either black or white. But he's not a bad guy.'

'I'm not a bad guy either! You know as well as I do that the "gentleman callers" are my language students. I teach them

English, and that is all.' She put her nose in the air and finished primly, 'I take exception to your Mr Burland's assumption that I am a Nazi sympathiser with the morals of an alley cat.'

'Still brooding over Mr Burland?' Hildegard was leaning on the side of the boat on the return journey, her back turned to the deck. Sam sat next to her and nudged her shoulder with his. She turned and looked at him but said nothing.

'You know,' said Sam, 'The last time I came sailing along here was on a boys' trip. I remember Bill was interested in the channel, and I told him about the water, like I was telling you earlier, and about the countercurrrent.'

'The countercurrent? What's that?' said Hildegard with grudging interest.

'In the Bosphorus, the current flows north-south, from the Black Sea to the Sea of Marmara and then out to the Aegean, right?'

She nodded.

'That's on the surface,' he went on. 'Beneath that, there's a countercurrent of deep water flowing in the opposite direction, toward the Black Sea. Not many people know about it, and you can't see it, but it's there, and it's strong and it reaches its goal.'

'Who would have thought?' said Hildegard.

'The thing is,' Sam went on, 'Bill didn't believe me. He said he knew the surface current was cold, and pretty powerful, and he couldn't imagine anything would succeed in going against it.'

'Just because you can't see it doesn't mean it isn't there,' said Hildegard.

'I know,' he said, holding her gaze. 'But I guess Bill's one of those people who only trusts what's in front of his eyes.'

She stared at him. How long has he known? she wondered. She gazed across at the spiked skyline of the European shore and breathed deep the salty air.

Chapter 25

'Good evening, Miss.'
'Good evening, Mac. Shall I go straight through?'
Hildegard's visits to the anonymous little house had fallen into a
familiar pattern. Mac's welcome inside the swiftly closed door
was followed by the sinuous tendrils of Gershwin's Rhapsody in
Blue swirling along the corridor, drawing her in toward the back
room. She had once mentioned it was a favourite of hers, and
since then it had become the soundtrack to her visits. Through
the winter, the fire was always lit, and a pair of satin slippers had
appeared by her chair, emerald green, another favourite, and
beautifully embroidered. A soft blanket had been draped over
the chair back, every consideration was made for her comfort.
Tonight there was need of neither fire nor blanket, as the
springtime tipped into summer, and Hildegard relaxed in her
chair. Her feet were burning from a long shift in Taksim's and
she was thankful for the soft, cool slippers. As usual, Mac

delivered the drinks tray, lit one of Sir's expensive cigarettes that she had fitted into her cigarette holder, and retreated.

'Not Bordeaux, then, Sir?' she smiled at him.

'No, it seems the landings in the Bay of Biscay were strictly notional,' he said, smiling back. 'But there's a long way to go yet.'

'I know. Still, I hope it helped a bit.'

'We may never know. We shall have to be satisfied that we did what we could.'

They were talking about the D-Day landings that had taken place a couple of weeks before. News had come that the German-occupied Normandy coast was not as well defended as it might have been, and they were hopeful that the rumour of an Allied invasion on the west coast of France, which Hildegard had relayed to Wolff, had been passed on up the line. She had not known the entire plan, but it was a deception operation called "Ironside", designed to make the enemy divert military resources to defend against a fictional American invasion in the Bay of Biscay, and away from the real invasion on the north coast. There were several such diversionary plans in operation for different targets around the French coast, across the Mediterranean and into the Balkans, under the umbrella of Operation Bodyguard, so named for Churchill's assertion that in wartime the truth was best protected by a bodyguard of lies. The truth, of course, being the actual D-Day invasion plans for Normandy. Perhaps the rumour that Hildegard had passed on had at least caused some doubt and confusion, if not significant military diversions. The boat trip picnic had been useful as an alleged source of this gossip, it was, she had told Wolff, the subject of an urgently whispered conversation between two senior consular officers that she had happened to overhear.

'I think he still trusts me, though, as much as he trusts anyone. He said today that he had heard the same plan from other sources, so there must have been some truth in it. I don't know who,' she mused, 'anyway, I don't think he's suspicious of me.'

'Good. Since the invasion, things are happening very quickly all over the continent. We need to be on our toes, but remember, it is my duty to tell you that if anything happens to you, we know nothing about you.'

After Hildegard left in the early hours, he sat a while longer in quiet reflection by the empty grate. His initial impression of her had more than proven correct, she had indeed been of great use to him. He had confirmed her status as a German agent in his reports to Cairo, and publicly she had played the part well. He had taken a risk in order to ensure that Wolff trusted her. No, if he was honest about it he would admit, if only to himself, that it was she whom he had asked to carry the risk, and she who would have, and would still suffer the consequences if she were exposed. In the months since, it had become apparent that so far it had paid off, Wolff trusted her, as much as he trusted anyone, and had swallowed whole her chickenfeed about Ironside, the notional Allied invasion operation on the west coast.

That was just a small part of what she had achieved. She had the most phenomenal memory and was able to read any open German documents on a desk, even upside down, and then relay the contents faithfully translated, hours later. Lately, she had even removed a few, when the opportunity arose, and humbly delivered them to him in this very room. There was no doubting her courage and he regretted having only the cold rejection of his warning to offer her in return, that she would not be recognised by the British if she were caught. It was a harsh but necessary precaution, which he hoped would never become reality.

Chapter 26

Istanbul, June 1944

Colonel Scarlat Urlateanu of the Rumanian Army General Staff manoeuvred his corpulent frame through the driver's door of his Ford Mercury and wound down the window. The car was a constant source of pleasure to Scarlat. It was majestically imposing, midnight blue with chrome trim that his man kept perfectly polished, and it turned heads everywhere it went. Scarlat considered it a most appropriate vehicle for a man in his position. He ran his eyes over the gleaming chrome around the dashboard dials and inhaled the familiar beeswax and leather scent of the interior. Yes, it was a car worthy of a senior diplomat. Settling himself along the front bench seat, he started the engine and pulled away from the German Consulate.

Scarlat drove north through the city, a couple of miles out to his favourite spot, by a hilltop park. From here he could see Pera below, the heart of European Istanbul, and the wide blue Bosphorus alongside it, a fellow exile from the shores of his homeland, flowing eternally by on its way to the Sea of Marmara.

He rubbed the bridge of his nose between his thumb and forefinger. It was the late afternoon of a very long day, and he was tired. He reflected on the conversation he had just had which, although unexpected, was most welcome. It had the potential to pull his life out of the nosedive it had taken lately. He had been offered an opportunity for some very important work and, if he were successful, it could be extremely gratifying.

The son of an old and distinguished Rumanian family, Scarlat had worked hard to honour his ancestors, and his country. Good school results, followed by the best military academy, an army commission and a solid military career, leading eventually to his posting here as Vice Consul in Istanbul. He had fulfilled his destiny, and he was proud of his achievements. Eighteen months ago, he had arrived in Istanbul as a man of consequence, fifty years old, distinguished, experienced, commanding respect.

But since then, what had happened? Somehow, since he had come here, things had started to go wrong. Wolff was to blame for some it, of course. They met at a reception in the German Consulate, when Scarlat had first arrived in the city, and relations had begun well sharing, as they did, the fascist ideology. Not quite, Scarlat corrected himself. His views were not quite the same as Wolff's. Wolff was an ardent Nazi, but he, Scarlat, was more refined in his views, more considered in his politics. He was right-wing, no doubt about that, but he was a nationalist, a defender of Rumania for the Rumanians. Not quite the same as a Nazi, in his view. But there was other common ground between him and Wolff. They held similar positions, each of them Vice Consul in Istanbul as cover for their work with their respective nations' intelligence services, and they even agreed between them a degree of friendly co-operation. Although looking back, it seemed to Scarlat that just as Rumania was subordinate to the Reich, so it had been more give than take for him in his dealings with Wolff.

After a few weeks at home in Bucharest back in the spring of 1943, Scarlat had returned to Istanbul and visited Wolff at the German consulate. It was then that he met the beautiful and charming Miss Goldacker. The thought of her made his heart soar. She was Wolff's new secretary, and the love of Scarlat's life, the most perfect woman he had ever met. He was determined to marry her, and he would, just as soon as his wife in Bucharest would grant him a divorce. Dear Miss Goldacker, how he missed her. Unfortunately, Wolff's puritanical sensibilities had meant he disapproved of their affair, and when they refused to break it off, he had promptly dispatched Miss Goldacker back to Vienna. It occurred to Scarlat that perhaps Wolff distrusted him, that was the real reason he objected to the relationship, rather than a superficial show of propriety over his marital status. Either way, she was dismissed and he had remained here, in utter despair.

Wolff had been decidedly cool toward him since then. Scarlat had tried to build a bridge by sharing with Wolff the news that he had previously been employed by the Abwehr, the German military intelligence, in Bucharest, with the full approval of the Rumanian Secret Service. He was prepared to offer Wolff information about internal Rumanian politics, providing Wolff had no qualms about blurring the line between Gestapo and Abwehr. The German civilian and military intelligence services invariably ran parallel without overlap, but Wolff considered Scarlat's offer acceptable, as long as they stuck to political matters and did not stray into military ones, which would remain the remit of the Abwehr. He would even pay Scarlat for the information, fifteen hundred Turkish lira a month, which was most agreeable, given Scarlat's penchant for the finer things.

Scarlat's first such report to Wolff was the revelation that there were politicians in Rumania that were less than totally committed to the Axis alliance. Wolff had seemed neither surprised nor impressed by this information, but it was a serious concern to Scarlat Urlatianu, very serious.

There could only be bad consequences if Rumania were to reject the Nazis. Firstly, the place was already swarming with feldgrau, it would be easy for the Reich to forcibly take complete control of the country, ending any illusion of Rumanian independence and sovereignty. The sovereign. Scarlat couldn't think about that now. That was an internal, infernal mess, and he needed to stay focused on the international picture.

The Nazis were unlikely to abandon Rumania, the rich Ploesti oil fields and the convenient coastal access to the Black Sea insured against that. But the Russians also had their eye on the valuable oil resource, not to mention the territory to be gained, so a political break with Axis would leave his country without an ally in the fight against the Soviets, and then with the Reich to contend with as well. A fight, ostensibly for the nation, but in reality for the oil, was almost inevitable on Rumanian soil.

It was unthinkable, intolerable for Scarlat that the Red Army would enter Rumania. But Scarlat was under no illusion that Rumania's connection with the Axis was guaranteed on either side. The domestic situation was unstable, there could be a Rumanian rebellion against the Nazis just as easily as the Nazis could turn on Rumania. Such chaos would make it easy for the Russians to march in. Regretfully, he had come to the conclusion that he would have to try to foster support elsewhere. If the Germans could not be trusted to protect his country from the Russians, then the only remaining option was the Western Allies. However unpalatable a surrender to them might be, it was the lesser evil if it meant the Soviets could be kept away.

Scarlat Urlatianu knew that Packy MacFarland worked for the American secret service. Everyone in Istanbul knew that, thanks to Gaden, the Czech pianist at the Park Hotel, who helpfully struck up a jaunty, Coward-esque rendition of a popular composition, "Boo Boo Baby, I'm a Spy" whenever one suspected of such activities entered the dining room, which was often. To his credit, Gaden was not partisan, and conferred this honour on the least discreet of the many intelligence officers and agents of every nationality then residing in the city, eliciting varying levels of humour in response. Packy was not a shy man, he would acknowledge Gaden with a smile and a wave and send him over a drink from the bar.

Boo Boo Baby, I'm a Spy

I'm involved in a dangerous game,
Every other day I change my name,
The face is different but the body's the same,
Boo, boo, baby, I'm a spy!

You have heard of Mata Hari,
We did business cash and carry,
Poppa caught us and we had to marry,
Boo, boo, baby, I'm a spy!

Now, as a lad, I'm not so bad,
In fact, I'm a darn good lover,
But look my sweet, let's be discreet,
And do this under cover.
I'm so cocky I could swagger,
The things I know would make you stagger,
I'm ten percent cloak and ninety percent dagger,
Boo, boo, baby, I'm a spy!

Lyrics credited to Leo Hochstetter
Music credited to Gaden

Scarlat had engineered discussions with Packy and got as far as agreeing to take an American radio set to Sofia for him, to be operated by an agent of the Bulgarian intelligence services. The purpose of the radio transmissions would be to relay to the Allies information such as the extent of the damage to the city following a bombing raid, and reports on German troop movements in the area, as well as to ingratiate Scarlat with the Americans. As insurance, he had offered Wolff the opportunity to colour these reports with alternative truths to send the Allies, but Wolff had been suspicious of the connection with the Americans and declined.

In the end, the whole enterprise was a waste of time. The radio set was destroyed in a bombing raid after only one signal was sent from Sofia, and now Wolff's distrust of him had deepened for his attempt to work with the Allies. Worse still, the Americans also distrusted him for failing to deliver. He had not managed to initiate a meaningful relationship with them at all, and his friendship with the Germans was in tatters. Instead of hedging his bets, he had found himself labelled as seriously duplicitous by both sides. The only benefit of the entire episode had been the four days he had stolen in Vienna with Miss Goldacker, as a detour of his trip to deliver the wireless set to Sofia.

To top it all, his masters in Bucharest had summoned him home, in early 1944, to explain his maverick connection with the Americans. He had refused to go, so they had relieved him of his Consular position, and with it his diplomatic status. Berlin had ordered Wolff to break relations with him too, and Scarlat had found himself completely isolated.

Scarlat's best efforts had come to nothing, and already the Red Army had marched over the border into his beloved homeland. While there was such uncertainty at home, as to where the nation's allegiance should be, he considered himself a political refugee. He knew what his own scruples were, and he knew they did not sit well back in Bucharest. Despite repeated orders to repatriate himself, neutral Turkey was the safer bet, and he was staying put, for the moment at least.

Scarlat had not seen Wolff for many weeks, but today he had been back in his office in the German Consulate. His meeting was not with Wolff himself, however, but his senior officer, visiting from Berlin, one Dr Schuback. Schuback had made it very clear that the task he was offering Scarlat was vitally important, and of the utmost secrecy. Not even Wolff was fully aware of the details. Did he think he was up to it? Scarlat had puffed out his chest at that, and humbly accepted the mission.

Chapter 27

Kiesewald, Silesia, July 1944

'Mama! Mama!' Erika charged up the street waving a letter in the air. Maria Braun turned suddenly at noise her daughter was making and spilled the bucket of water she had been delivering to the goats.

'My goodness, Erika, who has died?'

'What? Nobody,' Erika was flushed and breathless. She put her hands on her knees and gulped in air. Again she waved the letter at her mother.

'Klaus,' she gasped.

'Who's Klaus?' asked Eleanor.

Hedda rose from the back step where they were sitting in the sun.

'He's her boyfriend. She's got a boyfriend!' she sang, waggling her head from side to side.

'That's enough, Hedda,' said Mrs Braun with one of her pretend stern looks. 'What does he say, Erika?'

'He's got a week's leave, next month. And he wants us to get married!' Her squeal triggered a chain reaction of flapping and squawking, hugs and congratulations. Eleanor had never been to a wedding before but she thought they must be very exciting.

Preparations began immediately. Banns were read in church, and generous neighbours offered ration coupons to help with the celebration. Mrs Braun retrieved a dusty box from under her bed, and the girls and Anna watched as she took off the lid. She carefully peeled back layers of tissue and peered in anxiously, to see how her own wedding dress had fared during all these years in the dark. It was delicate, silk satin and lace, and when Erika held it against herself, her face was radiant.

'It's beautiful, Mama, are you sure?'

Mrs Braun nodded and wiped a tear from her cheek.

'Honestly, if I'm like this now, what will I be like on the day?'

Erika hugged her mother.

'Thank you. Just, thank you.'

The day before the wedding, Eleanor found Anna at the kitchen table, twisting the wedding ring on her finger.

'What's wrong, Grandma? You look sad.'

'I'm not sad, not exactly. I just wish we had something to give them as a wedding gift. Something special.'

Eleanor thought for a minute.

'You've made her dress fit, that's a kind of present, isn't it?'

It was true, Anna had worked her magic with the finest needle she could find, and now the mother's heirloom dress looked as though it had been created for the daughter. But there was no money to buy a proper present, and nothing to buy anyway. Anna was thinking.

'I know.' she said, 'Come on, you can help.'

She grabbed a basket and whisked Eleanor out of the house before she could ask where they were going, or what they were doing, and quick marched up to the meadow.

'See here, these are ripe, pick these and be careful not to squash them. These, look, they are still a bit green, leave them, they'll be sour.'

They worked their way around the low clump of bushes until the basket was almost full with chalky white-bloomed berries.

'Back to the kitchen now, we'll make them look special.'

Eleanor thought they looked lovely already. She wanted to try one but she daren't, not if they were somebody else's present. They sat at the kitchen table with a soft cloth each and polished the bloom off each berry until it shone like jet on a beach, then placed them carefully back in the basket, now lined with a crisp white cloth. Eleanor leaned over the basket, inspecting the berries and breathing in the sweet fragrance.

'They have little crowns, Grandma, and they smell like strawberries and roses.'

'They do,' Anna smiled.

The mountains blessed them with a perfect day for the wedding. Brushed, scrubbed, pressed and polished, Hedda and Eleanor shone in their best summer dresses. Anna, as a rule, subscribed to a peculiar Victorian notion that women over forty should always wear black, but with uncharacteristic joie de vivre, she threw caution to the wind for the occasion and put on her party navy blue.

The three of them walked down the lane and waited outside the church, with dozens of neighbours and well-wishers, to watch the bride arrive. Erika, accompanied by her mother, perched in the flower festooned buggy, and was ponderously delivered by the ancient horse in its jingling harness. Eleanor stared in wonder, seeing Erika in her wedding dress, surrounded with flowers, was like watching an angel descending, the most beautiful vision she had ever seen. Eleanor too had a role to play, and conscientiously held Erika's veil as she solemnly followed her up the aisle. Remembering to hold her head up and keep her back straight, deportment, Grandma called it. She thought she might burst she was so full of pride that she had been asked to be part of the wedding.

Later, the wedding feast was a genuine triumph over adversity, with food more abundant and delicious than anyone could remember. Everyone thought Anna and Eleanor's gift, the sweet gleaming gems in the basket, inky black against their white cloth, the most extraordinary blueberries.

A year had passed in the mountains. They had heard of the Allied landings in France, but news of the war was distant and the more immediate concern for people here was their own daily struggle. Occasionally, a little relief arrived for Anna and Eleanor, in the form of a carefully wrapped parcel.

'I know that smell, it's the woods, or, no, I know, it smells of Uncle Herman,' said Eleanor, inhaling the scent of the brown paper package they had just collected from the post office. But the package was not from Herman. A rare letter from Hildegard had found them, and rarer still, it was accompanied by precious goods to barter with.

'Tobacco,' said Anna with gratitude, when the parcel was opened on the table. 'Let's go down to the village later and see what we can get for this.'

The black market here in the mountains had always operated more openly than in Berlin. Perhaps because of the remoteness of the place, the people here had a natural resourcefulness and self-reliance, and a strong sense of community. They did what they needed to in order to get by and helped each other when they could. Still it was a meagre existence, and help from any quarter was welcome.

The letter accompanying the tobacco was brief and vague. Hildegard was well, and although things were tricky where she was, she thought she would be alright. She hoped they were well and sent all her love. Anna had no idea what she meant by 'tricky', but she had also said she was alright, so they should think of that. Eleanor sat wistfully looking at the letter, following the words with her finger, but Hildegard's writing in her signature green ink was too cursive for her to read.

Anna saw her dropped shoulders and bowed head and put down the sock she had been darning.

'Why don't you get your book, Eleanor? Shall we see what Klarchen is up to?'

Eleanor wriggled close to Anna on the sofa and opened the book across their laps. She flicked through listlessly, stopping at pages where Klarchen's mother was with her, usually reprimanding her for some mischief or other.

'Klarchen's mummy is cross with her again,' said Eleanor flatly.

'That's because Klarchen is a naughty girl, not a good girl like you.'

They looked at a few more pages, then Eleanor asked

'Why can't Mummy come to see us, Grandma?'

'She doesn't have permission, sweetheart, you need papers to travel.'

'Well, can we go and see her, then?'

'No, we don't have any papers either. I'm sorry.'

There was a silence and then Anna realised that the little body next to her was trembling. Eleanor was crying.

'Oh dear, what's the matter? Here, wipe your eyes.'

'What if Mummy forgets about us, Grandma?'

'She hasn't forgotten, come on now, she sent us a letter just today, didn't she? And a parcel to help us.'

'But, what if she does?' in a small voice she added, 'And, we forget her?'

'Is that why you're sad? Do you think you are forgetting her?'

Eleanor nodded miserably.

'Why? Why do you think that?' asked Anna gently, wiping Eleanor's face with her handkerchief. Through juddering breaths, Eleanor explained.

'Because sometimes when I think about her, it's not really her. I think she laughs all the time, and then I remember that's Mrs Braun, not Mummy. And I think she looks after me, but that's you, that's not her either. I even think she tells me off, but that's Klarchen's mummy in the book, and she's not even real.'

Her voice broke and she sobbed as Anna held her and gently rubbed her back. 'Mummy's getting muddled in my head, and smaller and further away, and I think soon she might be gone altogether.'

There were deep furrows between Eleanor's brows, the corners of her mouth turned down and tears flooded her cheeks. Her memories were distorting like a caricature, pulled wider by Mrs Braun's laughter, filled out by Anna's care, and sharpened by the discipline of the fictional Klarchen's mother. To Eleanor, her Mummy was becoming more and more like a character in a book. Real, but not real.

Chapter 28

Istanbul, August 1944

'Mrs. Reilly, Sir.'

'Thank you, Mac, show her in, would you?'

The Rhapsody in Blue unfurled to greet Hildegard as she followed Mac along the corridor toward the back of the house. She knew there would be a balloon of good brandy waiting and Sir, undoubtedly in his suit and tie despite the sweltering August heat which was relentless even in these small hours.

'Ah! Hildegard! Good evening. Come and sit down.'

'Good evening, Sir.' She accepted his invitation and the brandy wearily, as he sat in the armchair opposite, regarding her with his habitual interest.

'It's been quite a week, wouldn't you say?' the usual sparkle was absent from his eyes, his expression was sombre.

'Yes, Sir, it has.'

'And,' he continued carefully, 'have there been repercussions, so to speak, for you, as yet?'

'Yes,' said Hildegard dully, 'the Turkish police hauled me in a few days ago. I was supposed to get on a train to Germany the day after. Obviously I didn't go, but I'm worried they will find me. I'm hearing all sorts of things. Even Gaden has gone into hiding. You know the pianist at the Park? And he's not even German. It is all rather worrying.'

'Quite. Well, it is a particularly tricky situation for you. What have you heard?'

The war had moved on apace since the D-Day landings, and the tricky situation to which Sir referred was a consequence of Turkey's recent decision to cut diplomatic ties with Germany. It had become clear to the Turks that the Germans neither would, nor could, defend Turkey against a Soviet assault should the Russians continue their march south through the Balkans because of their own heavy military commitment in the north after D-Day. Not quite ready to side with the Allies completely, Turkey's only hope of preventing a Soviet invasion was to abandon its carefully sustained neutrality and make a gesture of goodwill to the Allies by cutting the diplomatic link with Germany. As a result, all German nationals were to return home immediately, German diplomats were to be interned pending an exchange for their Turkish counterparts currently in Germany, and asylum seekers would have to state their case and hope for clemency.

'I heard an awful story today which, if it's true, is terrifying.'

'Go on,' he said.

'One of the first trains that left had people on it who had asked for asylum here but been refused. I'm sure the Turks had their reasons for that, but nevertheless those people did not want to return to Germany. They had been here for years, some of them. And others, well, they were known to oppose the Nazis. It was almost as if the Nazis had chosen those people for the first transport, and maybe they did, somehow, influence that. In any case, they knew, Sir, the SS knew who was on the train, and as soon as the train was on Reich territory, they took them all off and…' Hildegard's voice caught, 'they shot them.'

He noticed the tremor in her hand as she raised her cigarette holder to her lips and took a long draw into the back of her throat. He nodded slowly,

'I heard that too. It seems the Germans did know who the asylum seekers were, and they clearly did influence the order of travel. It's a sorry business.'

'It is,' Hildegard said, and then added quietly, 'I could have been one of them. I could easily have been on that train, with my name included as one who does not want to go back to Germany.'

Sir understood the terror she felt at this event, and just how narrowly she had avoided it. But he but could offer her no reassurance, no security. She was, after all, unacknowledged. She was just a shadow in the background in his most secret world, for whom he need not account. But he was the first to admit she had been useful and could continue to be.

'Look, I'll see to it that your British passport is renewed, then you have legitimate papers to show if you are called in again by the Turkish police. And I'll have a word with Ferruh.'

'Ferruh?' Hildegard was confused at this. The only Ferruh she knew was a Turkish man who worked, as far as she was aware, as a translator for the press office in the German Consulate.

'Yes, that's him.'

'But he works for the Germans, actually in the German Consulate.'

'I know. I put him there,' said Sir, with a mischievous smile.

'Ferruh works for you, Sir?'

'Ferruh works for anyone that pays him. Actually, that's not entirely fair. I think he is a patriotic Turk at heart, and his own country's interests are of paramount importance to him. He works for them too, of course, the Turkish police, that is, and the intelligence service.'

'Well.' Hildegard took a moment to digest this information, then a terrible thought occurred to her.

'Ferruh could have leaked the list. I mean who knows where his sympathies really lie. If he works for the Turkish police he may have known who the asylum seekers were, he could have told Wolff and then Wolff gave the order to the SS. Wolff is still in the Consulate, they're not locked up yet, you know, he's probably still in contact with Berlin.'

'Yes, you may very well be right about that, I'm sorry to say. Ferruh does his best to nurture the unofficial relationship with Wolff and informing him of the asylum seekers would certainly have helped with that. And it is well within Wolff's capabilities to have organised a reception detachment from Berlin to meet the train in Vienna.' Sir agreed grimly. 'For the Turks, the number one enemy is still Russia, and the ideal solution for them would be a peace brokered between the Western Allies and Germany, at Russia's expense. Turkey may have severed their diplomatic ties with Germany, but they haven't thrown their lot in with us, exactly. Not yet anyway, while there's still a chance they'll need Germany's help against the Soviets. Ideally, they might show a little more commitment to their position, and there are a number of things we would like them to do differently, like rounding up the German diplomatic mission here a little quicker.'

'And not handing out lists of innocent people to be shot.'

'Quite. Ironically, I believe Ferruh has indicated to Wolff that if he himself, among others, were to apply for the Turkish right of asylum, they would receive a favourable response.' Hildegard turned her head away in disgust. She could hardly believe what Sir was saying. 'I am lead to understand that they declined. They prefer to retreat, presumably to do what they can from within Reich borders, so they are waiting to be repatriated. As I said, the Turks have sometimes chosen a different route from that which we would prefer. Unfortunately, I am not in a position to put any pressure on them, and the diplomatic wheels turn slowly, so this is where we find ourselves. I'd suggest you lie low for a while. Why don't you get out of town? Stay with friends in the country, perhaps?'

'No, a couple of people have kindly offered, but I want to stay here for now. I've moved out of my flat for the time being. Actually, I've sort of accidentally ended up at Sam's. There were Turkish police all over the place the day I was supposed to get on the train, so I took a roundabout route home, using the alleyways. Anyway, I could see the police outside my apartment and on the main road as I was coming back up the hill, so I took a detour away from there. Luckily I noticed a window open in Sam's apartment, so I climbed up the fire escape of the building next door, sneaked across the flat roof, and in through the window. I delivered myself rather inelegantly onto his bathroom floor.'

Sir laughed. 'And what did Sam have to say about that?'

'He wasn't in, fortunately, and by the time he got back I was a far less dishevelled fugitive. Anyway, I can stay there for now, and I've left Taksim's. The Germans might not be allowed out on the town anymore, but lots of other people are, and you never know who talks to whom.'

'Very wise. Do be careful, won't you?'

They sat in silence, Hildegard watched her brandy swell and recede as she gently swirled it around the bowl of her glass, thinking about Ferruh. He was a small, wiry man, with weathered skin and deep lines at the corners of his eyes. Sam said he was a spiv, because his black hair, streaked with silver at the temples, was oiled back and he wore sharp suits and patent shoes, but Hildegard liked him. He had always had a pleasant word for her whenever she ran in to him at the German Consulate. Now that she thought about it, the news that he also worked for the British made sense. Sir had always seemed to know when she had been to see Wolff, it must have been Ferruh who told him. And it was likely that Ferruh, among others, had reinforced the Bay of Biscay Allied invasion story to Wolff. But it was probably Ferruh too, who gave the names of the anti-Nazi Germans wishing to remain in Turkey to Wolff. In trying to preserve his nation from the hands of the Russians, he had sent those people to their deaths. Now she discovered that he had acted on orders to offer a safe haven to the Nazis remaining here. It was a sobering reminder to Hildegard to trust no-one. The fact that if she were caught, the British would deny any knowledge of her shadowed her every waking thought. She was on her own.

Chapter 29

Sir sat for a long time in the little parlour after Hildegard had left, deep in thought about this woman who had appeared out of the blue almost a year ago. He had been suspicious of her at first, of course he had, she was, to all apparent intents and purposes, the enemy. But it had very quickly become clear that her actual intents and purposes were most definitely on the side of the Allies.

The few reports he had sent to HQ in Cairo about her had been deliberately dismissive, writing her off as a German agent. He had never acknowledged her as sympathetic to the Allied cause, let alone of very great use to it. Which she certainly had been. She had proved herself time and again, bringing information, taking information, all at her own risk. A risk which, in recent weeks, had escalated considerably.

It was unfortunate that in order for her to be so successful in her work for him, she needed to remain publicly German. It had been a deliberate ploy of his, early on, to reinforce this perception. He had tucked her neatly into his reports between the usual array of undesirables, the smugglers and black marketeers, the propagandists and the collaborators, as a reported German agent, tasked with extracting information from indiscreet British and American visitors to the Casino Bar. The Germans were evidently and conveniently keen to exploit her attractiveness, her knowledge of English and her British passport to this end, and never questioned her motives or sources. Having established her German-ness, Sir had allowed her to fade into insignificance by dropping any mention of her from his reports in recent months.

It seemed to have worked. The rumours he heard in the Consulate stemmed from Bill Burland having taken a dislike to her, and why wouldn't he? As far as Bill was concerned, she was working for the Nazi's as well as in the Casino, and in Bill's eyes any woman that behaved that way, working in a bar, wearing make-up and the like, was surely some level of harlot. Personally he tended to agree with his wife, whom nobody would accuse of being anything less than ladylike, that meticulously applied lipstick and a discreet dab of Chanel No.5 were good for everyone's morale, and were absolutely no indication of loose morals. But Bill had decided that the German woman from Taksim's had dubious standards, and there was nothing he could say or do in her defence. Nor would he wish to. It suited him that the British colony at large considered her at best inconsequential, at worst even a Nazi sympathiser. Only he and the trustworthy, dependable Mac knew how committed she was in opposition to them. Privately, he considered her the best female agent in Istanbul.

It was no wonder then, his growing discomfort in leaving her so exposed. The German colony were in immediate danger of deportation and where Hildegard was concerned, that was potentially disastrous. He knew her to be quick witted and resourceful, she had evaded capture so far and things were happening so quickly across the European theatre now, if she could just hold on, he was sure this furore would blow over soon. He hoped so, it remained out of the question to show his hand and effect any kind of a rescue. He was not her guardian angel, he could not catch her if she fell, but he felt responsible, at least in part, for the peril she now found herself in, and he was rooting for her.

Chapter 30

'Chas is back!' said Sam excitedly, as he bounded into the apartment.

'Wonderful!' said Hildegard. 'Who is Chas?'

'Old friend, oil man, used to work at the British Consulate. He's been away in Rumania for months, and I can't wait to hear what he's been up to. I'm going to meet him tonight, it could be a late one.'

Sam was gathering pencils and notepads into his battered leather satchel as he talked. He kissed the top of her head and left again in a hurry, calling 'Don't wait up,' as the door slammed behind him.

'Looks like it's just you and me tonight then, Mr Mouse.' Hildegard put a bowl of food down for the dog and went to run a bath.

The influences that had shaped Rumanian culture were as rich as any. The language had a romantic Latin background, colour washed with hints of Turkish and Slavic that distinguished it from its more westerly cousins. As for the church, that fell within the spectrum of Byzantine Christian orthodoxy, and was consequently bound by fewer inhibitions than its Roman friends. The early twentieth century Rumanian intelligentsia were enthusiastically Francophile and wholeheartedly embraced French culture, from the Encyclopedist philosophers to fashion, from society suppers to the opera. By 1939, the chattering classes were still strongly pro-French and with a war looming, fully expectant of French protection against Russia, the treacherous enemy of ages who could on no account be trusted. The Rumanians did not trust Germany either, due to a complex precariousness of loyalties between motherland and kingdom for the Hohenzollern-descendent Rumanian royal family. When in 1940 the French could not defend themselves, let alone anyone else, against the might of the German army, it was clear that Rumania would need to seek other alliances. The populace may have preferred the Western Allies over Germany, but it would always choose Germany over Russia.

Early in the war, following the Dunkirk evacuation and the fall of Paris, morale in Rumania was low. The Rumanians felt isolated and vulnerable having been cut off from their friends. How could the Western Allies possibly help them now? The Rumanian government remained doggedly neutral but were undermined domestically by their own pro-German security service. The government tried too to maintain control over the direction of flow of the country's oil, but Rumanian economic dependency on Germany was irresistible, and it became apparent that Germany was the only realistic hope of protection against Russia, the greatest threat.

The Russians were demanding that Rumania cede large territories to them, and Germany urged them to comply. The Rumanians had strong suspicions of some secret skulduggery behind the Molotov Ribbentrop pact between Russia and

Germany at their expense but could not prove anything. The Rumanian army would be unable to defend against potential attacks from both Hungary and Bulgaria, on their western and southern flanks, as well as Russia to the north and east, so the government was forced to comply and cede the land to Russia, in order to preserve the other vulnerable regions of the country and avoid a total occupation, such as Poland had suffered.

The Rumanian government swelled with pro-Germans, and inevitably came to align the country with the Axis. King Carol requested that Hitler intervene to halt Hungarian and Bulgarian ambitions on his country, quid pro quo for having complied with his wishes over the Russian demands. But the Fuhrer was sympathetic to these nations, which had lost territories in the peace settlements following the last war and turned a blind eye as Bulgaria reclaimed their historic losses from Rumania.

Still the Hungarian threat remained. Hitler suggested to Mussolini that he should not support a Hungarian invasion of Rumania, on the basis that such action could severely compromise the supply of oil to Germany, and with the Rumanian defences now concentrated on the western front against such an invasion, there was no guarantee of success. A lengthy campaign here would risk drawing the Russians deeper into the Balkans. To the outrage of the average Rumanian, Hitler brokered the unopposed concession of lands by Rumania to Hungary as well. King Carol's ineffective protests were widely condemned as cowardly, and there were calls for him to relinquish his power as royal dictator.

The removal of the king would make way for Germany to instal a more biddable leader. On 5 September 1940, under pressure from Hitler, King Carol abdicated. His crown was bestowed upon his son, the new King Michael, who was quickly sworn in at the age of only eighteen, while his dictatorial powers went to a man called Antonescu, who took the fascist Iron Guard as his partners in the new National Legionary State government. Antonescu signed the Tripartite Pact with Germany and Italy, and Rumania was melded with the Axis.

Sam Pope Brewer, Oct.26, 1940: Istanbul:

"Turkey alone among the Balkan countries still offers real resistance to Germany's south eastward push, a rapid tour of the Balkan capitals has just shown this correspondent.

Greece has not yet really bowed but shows no prospects of serious opposition when the Germans and Italians are ready to act there.

The Balkans lie in the hollow of the German's hand. Yugoslavia, which a few months ago seemed a possible bulwark, now seems more likely to become an island in a sea of Nazi conquest, like Sweden in the north, and to be as completely dominated as Sweden without even a chance to fight. Hungary is going Nazi with gusto, though Admiral Horthy's regime keeps up the pretence of governing independently. And Rumania is almost a German colony.

The Germans have shown great skill in devising a special method for undermining each country by the tactics best adapted to the local situation. It did the Balkanites no good to study the methods used on their neighbors, because while they were doing that, they were attacked from a different angle.

Rumania, as the richest and weakest Balkan state, was the first, the most complete, and the easiest victim. The problem in each case was to get control in the form of co-operation, instead of resorting to force.

In Rumania's case, a horde of agents of all types, working patiently and industriously succeeded, with the German army as a club if they needed it, in swinging Rumania during the last year from an independent kingdom governed by a royal dictator and guaranteed by the
British, to a puppet country whose boy king rules only as he is told to rule.

When I arrived in Rumania a year ago, its sympathy was with the empires, though Germany's nearness made the country cautiously neutral, officially.

They gave Germany supplies reluctantly, and they failed consistently to keep up the deliveries the treaty called for. They even made efforts occasionally to stem the flood of German propaganda.

Now they not only have a flood of German publications of all sorts, but the Rumanian press devotes itself to praising the Axis to the skies and ranting at their opponents.

German troops guard Rumania's strategic points. German uniforms are seen all over Bucharest. German guns guard the wells from which oil is flowing to Germany at four times the volume of last spring, and

German officers are reorganizing and training Rumania's army while the

Rumanians suffer food restrictions so the Germans will have more to eat.

Nearly all British have already left the country because it is useless to stay. Others are leaving as they get their permits, which the British claim the Rumanians are delaying to keep Britons there as hostages until defences against bombardment of the oil refineries are completed.

Three main elements helped Germany's bloodless conquest of Rumania:

First, "Boring from within" by a corps of hundreds of skilled German agents cooperating with the Iron Guard and other pro-German elements.

Second, the threat of eventual attack and the spectacle of what happened to the countries who resisted, and

Third, the fear that if they did not play Germany's game and get her protection, the Russians would gobble them up. They preferred to be swallowed by Germany, and fear of Russia played a vital part in their willingness to actually have German garrisons in Rumania.

A big section of the population loathes the present German domination, but it is there to stay, unless somebody else downs Germany."

Chapter 31

'Good to see you, old man.'

'You too, Chas, you too.' Sam and Chas shook hands warmly, and set off for Packy MacFarland's flat, where Chas was staying. 'I have to say you're looking very well for an escaped convict.'

'I had sympathetic gaolers,' Chas smiled, but the months of stressful exhaustion showed around his eyes.

They talked into the early hours. Things had changed in Rumania since Sam had written his report on the Balkan situation four years before. The last months particularly, while Chas had been held captive in that country, had witnessed a series of critical events.

Since joining the Axis, Rumania had become an active participant in the German fight, particularly on the Russian front, where they contributed military resources in the hope of regaining the lost territories. Beyond that, Antonescu committed his army to supporting Hitler's invasion of Russia proper, thereby confirming Rumania's complete and peaceful subjugation by Germany.

There were still people in the country looking for ways to reverse the situation, and the government's popularity shrank further as Rumanian casualties on the Russian front grew. The German army was very present in Rumania, but as a selfish and ungrateful guest, not an enforcer. The fact that Rumania was a German ally, rather than an occupied territory, meant that there remained degrees of freedom that might otherwise have been lost and a group of moderate democrats had managed to secretly maintain contact with the western Allies.

An ambitious plan was forming. Single acts of sabotage against the Germans would result in acute reprisals and a general reinforcement of security. But an organised military coup, with credible leadership, could be a fatal blow to both the fascist government and the German presence in Rumania. There were risks, of course. The planning had to be perfect, the timing must be set for when the German military presence was at its lowest, and every person involved must be absolutely committed. If the coup failed, or if the army under a new democratic government could not hold back an aggressive German response until the Allies arrived, then Germany would occupy Rumania. There would not be a second chance.

Chapter 32

Sam returned home the following morning, filling the flat and waking Hildegard with the smell of fresh coffee and warm pastries.

'You were up early,' she said sleepily, 'or was it late?'

'Both. Didn't get much sleep, that's for sure.'

'Breakfast smells nice. Thank you,' Hildegard ambled over to the table, running her fingers through her hair. 'How was your friend?'

'Pretty good, considering he's been in a prisoner these last eight months.'

'What happened to him?'

Sam chewed a mouthful of pastry thoughtfully, considering where to begin. There was a lot he needed to tell her.

'You remember Bill Burland, from the boat picnic?'

'How could I forget? He was rather rude, as I recall.' Hildegard pulled her cup towards her with a scowl. Trusting the coffee to dissolve her morning sullenness, Sam ignored her and continued. 'Bill works for an organisation called the SOE, the Special Operations Executive.'

'I thought you said he was something to do with shipping?'

'That's his cover job. His main job is organising agents to go into the Balkan nations and support pockets of resistance, blow things up, make a general nuisance of themselves. Chas works for them too.'

'Is that what Chas was doing in Rumania? And he got caught?'

'Kind of. The original plan for Chas' mission was straightforward sabotage of German communications. But they were also trying to encourage a military coup lead by a democratic politician there, called Maniu. Chas lived in Rumania for a long time before the war, Maniu is actually a friend of his. He has popular support in the country, but he is a reluctant figurehead. The numbers supporting Maniu in key positions, in the government for example, have been steadily growing, and Marshall Antonescu didn't dare suppress them because Maniu is so popular in the country. Therein lay the chance that the quisling government could be overthrown, so Chas and couple of others went in last December to support the rebellion. Unfortunately for Chas, he also had the task of breaking it to Maniu that Allied backing for his coup was dependent on the unconditional surrender of his new government to all three major players, Russia included.'

'I don't suppose that sat well with anybody.'

'No, it didn't. Least of all Chas. Long story, but unfortunately the parachute drop went wrong, and Chas' group was captured.'

'They were lucky not be shot as spies,' said Hildegard pointedly.

'Well, the way Chas told it, the actual capture was a pretty amicable affair. He only really started to worry when they were handed over to Antonescu's people in Bucharest.'

'That's understandable, given the reason they were there.'

'Right. But Antonescu didn't react as you might think. He actually welcomed them and offered them the services of his Foreign Minister to act as legal brief for their interrogation by the Germans.'

'Gosh! How very odd. Why would he do that?'

'Well, Chas had told him that the mission was to help Maniu. It was a risk telling him, but as he offered the information voluntarily it lead the Marshall to trust him. After that, he promised to keep them under Rumanian guard to protect them from the Germans. I guess he was making a point about who's in charge there as well. But he was as good as his word, unbelievable though it might seem.'

'Though I suppose the planned coup was ruined,' said Hildegard.

'Well, the planned one was, but a coup has happened.'

'What? There's been a coup in Rumania? How did I miss that?'

Hildegard prided herself on keeping up to date with the news but could not remember hearing anything about a coup in Rumania.

'You didn't. It only happened a couple of days ago, and you've been holed up here. I guess the news hasn't caught up with you yet. In the end, it was the young King who took the initiative, he's effectively taken charge, denounced the Axis and surrendered to the Allies, all of them. It was a Royal coup, no less.'

'Good for him,' she said, impressed. 'What a story.'

'That's not quite everything,' Sam said slowly. 'The thing is, it's a critical time in Rumania. Things are changing fast and they need a voice, someone to tell the world what's going on there. I have to go.'

The thought had been lurking in the back of Hildegard's mind that Sam would want to go, he would need to go and report from Rumania. There was too much going on there for him to sit on his hands here in Istanbul.

'When?' she said resignedly.

'Soon. A couple of days at the most. You know my friend Packy Macfarland?'

Hildegard nodded.

'The well-known American spy,' she said drily, thinking of Gaden at the Park Hotel.

'Well, he works for the OSS office here, that's the Office of Strategic Services, it's the American version of SOE,' Sam told her.

'Oh. So he really is a spy, then.' No surprise there.

'Yes,' Sam said slowly, rubbing his chin.

'What?' Hildegard narrowed her eyes slightly in mock suspicion, 'what haven't you told me?'

'The owner of my newspaper, The Chicago Tribune, is a friend of William Donovan, who is in charge of the whole OSS show.'

'So?'

'So, I have a part-time job, alongside reporting.'

'You work for this OSS, with Packy?' This was news to Hildegard.

'Well, strictly speaking I work for the SOE, with Bill and Chas, the OSS office is relatively new here, and I've been at it a while now. But we're pretty closely tied, yes.'

Sam poured them both more coffee as Hildegard pushed crumbs into a pile on her plate with her finger, thinking about what he had said. When she had overheard Bill Burland's conversation at the picnic, he had said that Sam was "one of ours". So this is what he meant. It was a lot to take in. Sam was certainly suited to covert work. He blended naturally into a crowd, never drawing attention to himself yet observing every detail of what went on around him. He was an able communicator too. Hildegard thought his pieces for the newspaper were written with insight and clarity. But being an SOE agent put him in a very different position from being a reporter, if he were caught. She was acutely aware of the consequences that could bring.

'Sam, you remember when we first met, you told me a story about nearly getting yourself shot by a firing squad? In Yugoslavia, wasn't it, a few years ago? They thought you were a spy.'

'Yes,' his sheepish grin told her everything she needed to know. She did not raise the question about his imminent trip to

Bucharest. They sat in silence for a few while, each immersed in their own thoughts, until Sam said,

'Look H, I am a little worried about you while I'm not around, you will be careful to lie low for a while won't you? It's still pretty fraught out there, with the German deportations and everything.'

'I know. I will, don't worry,' she hoped she sounded reassuring.

'Well, Packy might be moving on soon too, but he's promised to look out for you while I'm away, for as long as he's in Istanbul.' Then, watching her carefully, he added, 'And your friend at the British Consulate has too.'

'My friend?' Hildegard could not think who he was talking about. Then it dawned on her, 'Sir? You mean Sir?'

'That's how you know him, yes.'

'You know Sir?' Hildegard was incredulous. Sam's revelations so far had been surprising, but this was bordering on surreal. 'I mean he knows who you are, I've told him about you, but I had no idea you actually knew each other.'

'Ours is a small world,' Sam shrugged. 'He's concerned for you, that's all. Same as me.'

'That's nice of him. I don't even know his name.'

'No,' said Sam, 'I know.'

He finished his coffee, and then left to keep an appointment at the British Consulate. After he had gone, Hildegard sat for a long time contemplating the morning's news. It seemed that everyone in Istanbul was spying for one side or the other. Or both, or even three, she thought of Ferruh. What an extraordinary place this was. And what about Sir? He had obviously talked to Sam about her, so that was how Sam knew about her own part-time work too. She wondered when had he found out. Had he known last year, before they had even met? Had Sir asked him to keep an eye on her, before she knew either of them? Is that why he was at Taksim's the night they first met? She had no idea how closely interwoven her connections were, nor whether she was right to trust them. She believed that Sir and Sam had both been as honest with her as circumstances allowed and that on a personal level, if she needed them, they would try to help her if they could. But there was no guarantee that either would be able to. Sir had never once failed to remind her of her position as far as he was concerned, that if she were caught she would be on her own. And now Sam was leaving Istanbul. It seemed to Hildegard that she was discovering the extent to which her own secret network was entwined just as it was beginning to unravel.

Sam flew to Bucharest a few days later. He had found it difficult to pack, not knowing when or even if he would return. His last night was spent needlessly moving things, packing, unpacking, repacking, drinking vodka alternated with coffee made by a listless Hildegard, who wandered around the apartment, lost.

Chapter 33

A week later, when Sam was entertaining the King of Rumania's private secretary to dinner in Bucharest, Hildegard was also dining with a Rumanian. They had been on polite nodding terms from Taksim's, where she had known him as one of Wolff's cronies. He was the older, self-important one in his antiquated officers' uniform, with its red tipped lapels and burnished buttons. The invitation to dinner had come as rather a surprise, Hildegard had never really had a conversation with this man and she wondered why he had asked her. She could only assume that he just wanted some company, now that his friends in the German legation were, at last, interned.

She did not know much about Rumania, other than what Sam had told her, but there seemed to be a lot going on there at the moment. It might be interesting to find out more about the place where Sam had gone. She remembered she had liked those people she had met from the Rumanian Embassy in Berlin, and that they had been kind enough to help her when she needed a visa. She doubted that he would be like them though, given the company he kept. In any case, an otherwise empty evening would be filled at least.

His man opened the door and with a silent scowl lead her in to a grand and graceful apartment, with tall windows, polished floors and a marble fireplace. The valet-chef spoke only Rumanian, and gruffly indicated her presence to his master before heading back to his domain, the source of the delicious aromas permeating the apartment. Scarlat was resplendent in his habitual dress uniform, which he was admiring in a huge wall mirror as she arrived. On the table, Ambassadorial settings with gold rimmed plates, a broad array of silver cutlery and crystal glasses on a pure white damask tablecloth all sparkled importantly in the light from an ornate silver candelabra. It was a scene demanding perfection, and dinner did not disappoint. Unexpectedly, from the appearance of its creator, the food was the finest French cuisine, beautifully presented and it tasted exquisite.

'He might look like a peasant, but he knows how to cook,' said Scarlat.

'He certainly does. This is a delicious meal, really superb.'

'I'll pass on your compliments to the chef.'

'Yes, please do.'

Scarlat put down his knife and turned to her.

'So, my dear, what brought you to Istanbul?'

'I was living in Berlin, but it was getting more dangerous, you know, with the bombing, and the opportunity arose, so here I am,' Hildegard said evasively. She had no wish to divulge more information about herself than necessary and guessed correctly that he would rather talk about himself anyway. 'And you? You are the Rumanian Vice Consul here, is that right?'

'Yes, the Vice Consul. At least, I was, until very recently.'

'Oh?' she said.

He dabbed at his mouth with a pristine white serviette, and drank some wine, never taking his black, rats eyes off her.

'I seem to have a different,' he paused, searching for the right word, 'perspective, to that of my government of late.'

'How so?' now Hildegard was interested. When she told Sir about the dinner invitation, he had been keen for her to accept. He told her that Urlateanu was a rogue agent, pursuing some untold mission all his own, and he wanted to find out what he was up to. She could guess where Urlateanu's sympathies lay from his friendship with Wolff and his open admission of discord with the new post-coup regime in his home country. Her task was to find out the specifics of his current activity. Fortunately, Scarlat needed little encouragement to launch forth on his favourite subject.

'What do you know about the Legion, the Iron Guard?' he said.

'Very little, I'm afraid.'

He pushed back his chair a little, relishing the opportunity to educate her.

'Allow me to enlighten you.'

His eyes shone with passion for his subject. He would take full advantage of his chance to talk about it. 'After the last war, there was a growing feeling of concern in my country, about the general spread of communism. We Rumanians are a proud nation, a Christian nation of traditional monarchists, we don't believe in communism, or any kind of dictatorship. Particularly as most of the communists seem to be Jews. Naturally, we turned instead to nationalism to protect ourselves. Many nationalist groups formed, and eventually they were united by a great man, a great leader called Codreanu, under the banner of The Legion of St Michael the Archangel, The Legion, as it became known, or the Iron Guard, which had been the name of one of the founding groups.' He drew a deep breath, he was into his stride now.

'Legionairism is based on seven founding principles, which I do believe have been distorted, and misunderstood in recent times. But I think you will find the nuances fascinating, as do I.'

Hildegard was paying full attention and nodded encouragingly, 'I'm sure,' she said.

'First, there is the nation, defined on the basis that the people of the world are not all the same. No, they are distinct from one another according to their nation. A nation, you see, is both a territory, and a people, identified by their shared national history, their language, culture, traditions and, naturally, a common destiny. Any nation such as this is a gift from God, and that commands respect.'

'I see,' said Hildegard. Scarlat did not hear her, entranced by his own narrative he ploughed on.

'Then, there is race. This is different from nation, in that it defines only the biological make-up of the people. But it is important, because in order for the nation to thrive, the race of the people must not be compromised by the introduction of other races, it must remain pure.'

Hildegard felt an uncomfortable anticipation of was coming next, then a flicker of the old emotion she had felt in Berlin, the hate that had provoked her into action and lead her to Istanbul. Her revulsion with fascism had not dwindled and Scarlat's beliefs were sounding horribly close to it. Somehow, she managed to maintain an outward appearance of polite interest.

'But we are not racist.' That was not what she had expected. Scarlat leaned forward and wagged a stubby finger at her.

'No, that is where we differ in ideology to the Nazis, we do not believe that other races are inferior to us. Not at all. We respect other cultures, of course. We just do not want to encourage immigration or intermarriage, to the detriment of our nation, that is all,' he said, convinced by his own voice of reason.

Hildegard held her fixed smile, but internally she was howling. What was the difference? The discrimination he had convinced himself was rational was indistinguishable from racism in her mind. The acceptance of prohibitive differences was exactly the spark that had ignited the horrific bloody firestorm that was this war. She would have found his ridiculous delusion, his twisted logic laughable, had it not been so chilling.

The chef-valet shuffled in to remove their plates and refill their glasses before withdrawing once more to his kitchen.

'Which brings me to the Jewish question.' Scarlat was watching her, but she was playing her part well. He was pleased by her apparent interest in his creed and continued.

'The Jews clearly should not be in Rumania. They are culturally and racially alien, a fact proven by their failure to assimilate in our society. They can only dilute our nation and they have absolutely no right to do so.'

'So, how do you think that might be resolved?' ventured Hildegard, a little afraid of what he might say. News of the true purpose of the concentration camps as factories of death was filtering through to Istanbul, as it was to the rest of the world, and Hildegard was naturally appalled at the scale of the evil. It was beyond imagining. Scarlat looked triumphant, as though he alone had found a solution to this most awkward conundrum.

'I think they should have their own nation. Send them all to Palestine, that's the best way. We Legionnaires have high moral standards, Christian standards. Codreanu exalted us to be "wiser, purer, more diligent and more heroic" than other men. We should be prepared to lay down our lives for Rumania, as he did himself, in the end. So let the Jews have the opportunity to do the same for a nation of their own. Except, it wouldn't be a Christian nation, of course,' he chuckled at his own observation, then allowed himself a self-satisfied smile at the generosity of his plan.

'Well, Christian values are indeed admirable,' Hildegard said diplomatically then, wanting him to move on, asked 'What else does a Legionnaire believe in?'

'Ah,' he said, his small dark eyes glistening with fanatical fervour, 'this is where it gets really fascinating. We have a highly advanced and intelligent ethos on political structure, it is truly inspired. Codreanu was a genius, in my opinion. The party's structure is not very different from many others, in that we have small community level groups, called cuibs, linked together into larger town and regional groups. But the genius is in the selection.' He stabbed the tablecloth with his forefinger to emphasise his point. 'Codreanu denounced democracy on the grounds that it does not guarantee good leadership, in fact often the best leaders are not elected to power. Instead, we get populists who manipulate the masses with their election promises, and once elected, seek only to serve themselves. The worst manipulators, by the way, are those with wealth and economic influence, and we know who that is, don't we? We should never have granted them citizenship, it can only worsen the undermining of our nation.'

He had contradicted himself, in accusing the Jews of democratic political machinations, having only minutes previously labelled them all communists. You're not showing much cultural respect now, are you? she thought, but she allowed him to continue unchallenged.

'In any case, democracy only encourages differences of opinions, and that is divisive, and then we end up with opposing factions within the nation, and constantly changing leadership, whereby nothing of any lasting value is achieved. Look at any democratic country and you will see evidence of that.'

'How then, do you select your leaders? If they are not voted in by the people, how are they appointed?'

'Exactly that, my dear, you catch on quickly. Our leaders are appointed, by other high-ranking leaders, on the basis of evidence of their ability to lead, and of their good character. We have wise and experienced men making rational choices. That is the genius of Codreanu. Enlightenment worthy of Voltaire, don't you think?'

Scarlat interpreted Hildegard's laugh as agreement, but it was a laugh of dark amusement at the irony worthy of Voltaire. She was sure that Voltaire himself must be turning in his grave at Scarlat's comparison between his philosophy and the Legion's code. The blatant religious intolerance inherent in the latter was the very opposite of enlightened.

Scarlat sat back and rolled the delicate crystal stem of his wine glass between finger and thumb of his thick, square hand, self-satisfied and replete.

'But what about at the very top then, is that one person or a committee? You mentioned you were monarchists,' said Hildegard, 'so, do you support the king?'

The flame of Scarlat's fervour was reignited by her question. The sovereign.

'Ha! That upstart? Absolutely not. He thinks he can rule the nation.'

'He is the king,' Hildegard pointed out.

'King he may be, but he is barely more than a boy, he has no right to throw his weight around like he has been doing. Look where that got us. He thought his puppet Maniu would dance to his tune, and the Western Allies would welcome him with open arms. They did not. They will not. And now we are swamped with Communists.'

'Tell me, then, what would be the Legion's solution? What would Codreanu do?' He had become rather heated at the mention of young King Michael, but to her relief, his eyes lit like those of the faithful at her question, and he was guided back on track like a docile mule.

'Codreanu. Good question. Yes, he had a solution alright. This was his genius. Listen, you will see it, I am sure. Codreanu most certainly supported the monarchy, far preferable to having some power hungry republican or communist dictator at the top. But the king should act in the best interests of the nation, and do whatever he must, not whatever he wants. Of course, he would be guided in this by the senior Legion leadership. So you see, we would have a traditional monarch, whose birthright it is to be the figurehead of the nation, but he would be advised and supported by the wisest and most able leaders. It is perfect, don't you think?'

Before she could respond, he went on.

'But young King Michael got it all wrong. He thought he would lead the nation himself and rely on Maniu to deliver his promises. He should have taken advice from those older and wiser than he. But no, he chose to act on his own impulse, the young fool, and look where we have ended up.' He shook his head sadly.

Since the King had effected his coup in Rumania and surrendered to the Allies only weeks before, the Red Army had flooded south through Rumania, and were now heading west.

Soon, Scarlat's worst fears would be realised and his country would be completely overrun by the Russians.

The chef returned to clear the last of the dishes, and Hildegard acknowledged him silently, leaving Scarlat to wallow undisturbed in his sorrows.

'Thank you,' she said eventually, 'it has been a most interesting evening. I do hope you will share your vision for the future of your country with me sometime, your views are truly fascinating.'

Chapter 34

'Good girl,' said Sir, an hour later, after she had faithfully relayed the details of the evening's conversation to him. 'So he has invited you back, that's excellent.'

Hildegard had found the evening rather draining. She was only glad that it was outside of her remit to challenge Scarlat.

'I'm not looking forward to another lecture. I think he's pompous and narrow minded, which strikes me as a rather cowardly combination, and frankly quite a stupid position to take. Luckily, according to Peter, there probably isn't much left for him to tell.'

'Peter?'

'A Hungarian friend, he's very interested in the politics of his Balkan home and neighbours, so I've had a couple of general discussions with him, just to gain a bit of background knowledge. Don't worry, Sam knows him too, he is definitely not a Nazi sympathiser and he has no idea of the real reason I asked him about it.'

Hildegard had continued her friendship with Peter and liked him enormously. He was an energetic young man and a committed student of history, as well as endeavouring to learn Turkish as well as English. He was passionate about the history of the region, and vividly described to Hildegard how nations had been formed from two main imperatives. First, the rise in the collective consciousness against the unfairness of aristocratic empirical rule with its "one rule for the gods, and another rule for the cattle" double standard philosophy. Second, the necessity of solidarity between small states against the perceived common threats to territory and sovereignty. Rumania had defined itself by the consolidating the states of Transylvania, Walachia, Moldavia and Bessarabia, and the deliberate development of a national cultural awareness so that Rumanians understood what it meant to be a Rumanian.

'All right. I can see that might be helpful to ask the right questions of Urlateanu but suggest you don't pursue it too hard with your friend, we don't want to arouse any suspicions.'

'No, Sir, I won't.' Hildegard trusted Peter but she was careful always to adhere to the rule of secrecy for everyone's protection. She turned her attention back to Urlateanu. 'I don't know how much more Scarlat will tell me but he does like to talk. Once he gets going it's quite hard to get a word in, actually. He seems quite sad, and I'm not sure if that's because of the state of his country, or just because he's lonely,' Hildegard reflected. Sir nodded slowly.

'Either way, you can exploit it, just by listening to him. It sounds as though he appreciates an audience for his pet topics. He's an egotistical character, you can tell by the way he struts around like Goring in his ridiculous dress uniform and has his man polish that enormous car to within an inch of its life.' Sir said, adding as an afterthought, 'The car, by the way, is a bit of a problem, as is the grand apartment.'

'Why is that?'

'Both relics of his diplomatic career. You've seen the CD plates on the Mercury? He might be persona non grata in the Corps Diplomatique, but as long as he lives his life between the car and the apartment, which is also still Rumanian consular property, so both have immunity, the Turkish police can't touch him. He has lost his diplomatic status, but his status symbols have not.'

'What is it they want him for?'

'He's up to something and the Turks want to know what, just the same as we do. He drives up to the hills most afternoons, sends messages from a wireless set. We've intercepted them, of course, but so far we haven't been able to decrypt them, so it's a mystery who is bankrolling him. Or why.'

Hildegard reflected on the sentiments of her earlier encounter.

'He was very nostalgic for a Legionary run Rumania, not surprising that he doesn't want to go back there at the moment, really. Perhaps he's working with some underground group back home, planning to rise up and overthrow the communists?'

'It's possible, but I think our friends in Bucharest would have heard something about that.' Sir watched the firelight's flickering gold reflection dancing in his brandy. 'I can see he tries your patience but keep going with this as long as you can, you are best placed to draw him out.'

Chapter 35

The necessity of the reminder that Hildegard was unacknowledged and unprotected still weighed heavily on Sir, but he diligently delivered it as was required of him. Again, he remained sitting in the darkened room after she had gone, deep in contemplation. His recent trip to Cairo had provided plenty of food for thought.

He had hitched a ride on a military flight which gained in expediency what it lost in comfort over his preferred route overland on the Taurus Express. There was neither restaurant car nor cushioned sleeper cabin, in fact no upholstery of any description on the transport plane, but it flew fast and high, taking a direct route avoiding the ack-acks on the islands, and arrived safely in a matter of hours rather than days. Emerging from the plane, the heat had hit him immediately, it was more intense here than Istanbul, where the fire of high summer had passed its peak. The taxi driver had tapped the side of his nose and nodded knowingly when he gave HQ's address.

'Yes, Sir. Secret building. I know it.'

HQ was in the haphazard residential district known as Garden City. There was some respite from the sun here, beneath the palms and tamarisks and acacias that threw their welcome shade across the winding streets and he found the greenery pleasant. It was not as lush as England, but to his eye it was preferable to the sand-scape that stretched from the city to the horizon in all directions. He paid the driver outside Grey Pillars, the secret building, and crossed the road to HQ's new home.

The acquisition of more spacious accommodation had inevitably followed the enthusiastic and exponential development of the secret war that caused HQ to burst the seams of its original home. Their new home was formerly a hotel of dubious repute. The ladies who lived and worked in the building agreed good-naturedly to contain themselves on the upper floors, so the two ancient and shadowy professions co-habited amicably.

The meeting to which he was called on this occasion was to discuss the continued expansion in activities that had necessitated the move. The Allied invasion had pushed on since D-Day forcing the Germans to retreat out of France. The Russians were progressing from the east and had reached the banks of the mighty Vistula outside Warsaw, and to the south they had swept through the newly cooperative Rumania on their way to complete dominance in neighbouring Bulgaria, Yugoslavia and Hungary. The momentum in the war was with the Allies, and SIME itself had once shared the ambition of reaching Berlin.

It was clear though that SIME's limited resources had been overstretched in trying to operate in the Balkans, as well as the Middle East. The primary function remained, of course, Security and Intelligence in the Middle East and it was time to regroup. Responsibility for SIME activities in south east Europe would be transferred to their counterpart in the Mediterranean theatre, and there would be a general reshuffle of personnel both in Cairo and across the region.

He left the meeting knowing that his own operations would be significantly affected, Istanbul being the major base as it was for activities in the Balkans. He was interested to see what the outcome would be for him and wondered where he might possibly be sent next. He stepped out of the building lost in his own speculations and was almost run over by a speeding Abdu, the trusty Egyptian who guarded the place proudly. He scooted around on a low wooden trolley on small wheels, apparently unimpaired by his lack of lower limbs.

'Watch out, Sir!' he called as he manoeuvred expertly around him.

'Sorry, Abdu,' he said to Abdu's fast disappearing back, 'I was miles away.' And may very well end up there.

Chapter 36

The weeks passed and the still warm breezy days ended swiftly with the damp scent of chill autumn evenings. The leaves had adopted their farewell blaze of colour, curling and twisting as the life gradually drained from them. The shape of Hildegard's days had changed too, now that she no longer worked at Taksim's and Sam had gone. She became a daytime creature once more, teaching her English students and seeing friends to fill her time. The best time of the day for her was the early morning, when she and Mr Mouse took long walks past the palaces and mosques close to the Bosphorus shore. They turned and walked uphill into the wooded city parks, randomly following the miles of trails that criss-crossed through them. Mouse ran in circles, investigating scents and chasing unsuspecting pigeons and squirrels, fully alert to the waking world. The brittle crunch of dried leaves and twigs underfoot and the tranquil freshness of the air drew Hildegard back to her childhood, and walks along the canal path in Neuss, or before that the river in Cologne. She felt the endless possibility of those days, when she could walk for hours, immersed in the sky and the sun on her face, the feel of the ground underfoot, the clear air filling her lungs, and the trees, always the trees. Every day a fresh sheet of paper, for her to fill as she wished. The days before the adult world had arrived, along with all its obstacles and challenges. Her companion in those days was her little dog Orno, long since departed, but somehow here with her in spirit, she could almost see him, scampering after Mouse. She imagined he had found her here, just as she had found herself again.

On the evening of her next dinner with the Rumanian she arrived at the apartment on time, and the chef-valet opened the door, ushering her in like a much missed relative and beaming a mildly alarming gap-toothed grin at her. Clearly nothing had been lost in the translation of her praise for his cooking.
Scarlat had started drinking already. He greeted her from his seat at the table, the dark dregs in his glass were the ominous remains of a bottle of wine. The meal was served promptly, along with another vintage bottle and more of the chefs own inimitable smiles. Scarlat focussed his attention on the bottle, and Hildegard was worried that any potential gains to be made tonight might drown, but he turned out to be a wistful and garrulous drunk, easily set back on the path he himself had begun at their last encounter.
'You were telling me before, I recall, about the principles of your Legionary Movement. Now I've had time to think about it, I wonder how you see a country, your country, operating under such a system?'
He pouted his lower lip and moved his head slowly from side to side, trying at once to focus his eyes and process her words. She pressed on.
'My question, I think, is about your dream for your country. What will it be like to live in your Legion's Rumania?'

Sir was right, he was egotistical, and nothing fed that ego better than the opportunity to share his inspired vision for his beloved homeland with an apparently captivated audience.

'Ah, Rumania. My Rumania,' he gazed into the distance watching himself, through an alcoholic haze, triumphantly returning to a Legionary Rumania. He saw his beautiful car sweep down the winding, wooded slopes of the Transylvanian Alps, to pass majestically by peasants toiling happily under a blazing sun in the baked brown fields of Walachia. They would down their tools and wipe their hands on their smocks to stand and watch respectfully as he passed. The people had once embraced Legionary ideology, and they would again see the perfection of its principles, he was sure of it. He would himself become one of the elders of the movement and offer his benevolent guidance to a contrite and biddable king in the service of the nation. He saw himself leave the pastoral idyll behind and enter Bucharest, his hometown, his beloved city. A city as elegant and refined in both architecture and inhabitants as any on earth. A city to rival even Paris in its beauty and brilliance. The car rolled slowly along the wide boulevards, where the best of society sat at tree-shaded cafe tables and Scarlat inclined his head graciously in acknowledgement of their greetings. He waved at the beautiful and doubtless irreproachably chaste girl leaning on the wrought iron balcony of her tall first floor window, the gold crucifix at her throat glinting in the sun as she waved back at him. The city was named for joy, and that is what it gave him.

'That is a place populated by a brotherhood of true Rumanians, each devoted to the nation, and confident in the righteousness and wisdom of the elite to lead them in the right direction,' he told Hildegard, slurring slightly. 'It is a peaceful place, where we work with honour for the good of the nation. We value honesty, and do not try to rob each other blind, like the damn Jews. No, we are law-abiding, Christian, peaceful people. But don't cross us, don't attack our nation.' He brought his gaze down from his reverie and wagged his fat finger at her. 'Don't make that mistake, for then, we are not peaceful. No. Then, we will fight,' he thumped his fist on the table, 'we will defend our country without mercy. Nothing challenges the importance of the nation, not family, not business, not religion, nothing. We lay down our lives for Rumania. Many have already been martyred in this cause, and their legend lives on. It is glorious! Glorious!'

He finished with an emphatic flourish which knocked his glass over onto his plate with a crash and brought the man running from the kitchen. There followed a heated exchange in Rumanian, which to Hildegard's ear had similar rhythms and intonations to Spanish. She spoke neither of those languages and could make neither head nor tail of what was being said, but it was clear that it was an argument. Just like an old married couple, these two, she thought. She made her excuses and left early. Her apathy toward Scarlat had turned into exasperation and the whole evening had been a waste of time.

Chapter 37

After the disappointing monologue which shed no light on
Scarlat's current activities, Hildegard was despondent for a day
or two. She was dissatisfied with her lack of progress in
discovering his activities and frustrated that her thoughts were
trapped in circular motion, perpetually returning to where they
began. She needed to break the pattern but could not think how.
To cheer herself up, she took the tram along Iskitlal Caddesi to
Galata and wandered down to the Golden Horn. She joined the
crowd whose daily business involved swarming to and fro across
the Galata bridge and felt the pontoon's gentle motion up and
down beneath her feet as it rested on the water. In Eminönü, she
headed south and up the hill to Sultanahmet and the Topkapi
Palace.

Hildegard could not have explained why she was drawn toward
the Palace that day. It was a beautiful place to visit, certainly,
but she had been there before and admired the gardens and
courts, the exquisite tiles and cool marble walkways. Today,
once inside the main gate she headed left, toward the rooms of
the harem. Still unable to articulate a reason, even to herself, she
wandered slowly along the passageways, their high pale stone

walls leaving just a narrow strip of sky as a view. Eventually, Hildegard came to a chamber, slightly larger than most, and distinguished by its simplicity. There was no one else around so she sat in solitude on a low bench and contemplated this place. The walls were white and had been decorated with a light touch, delicate depictions of fruit and flowers, painted in pale shades of green and pink, a restful, feminine contrast to the busy intricacies of the rest of the palace walls.

Hildegard had read about the harem when she first visited the palace. She had previously assumed that the women who lived here throughout the centuries had been slaves. Protected, yes, the Black Eunuchs saw to that, but restricted too, and entirely subject to the will of the Sultan. She had thought that they were powerless victims of their situation, forced to live their lives in this guilded cage.

She sat a while longer, held still in the tranquility of the harem. Hildegard remembered more of what she had read about it. That although many of its inhabitants were, of course, unfortunates who had suffered miserable existences within these walls, that was not true of all of them. Some of these women had translated their confinement into sanctuary, a place of privacy. Some of them had used their connections to gain considerable influence in the Palace, the city, even the entire the empire. They were unseen by the public eye, but powerful all the same. Perhaps that was why she had come here. Perhaps she felt some solidarity with those women, the ones who had been able to turn adverse circumstances to their advantage. They were countercurrents too, she mused, unsuspected, known to only a few and stronger than any would expect.

A card arrived from Scarlat, inviting her to dinner once more. This time she arrived early, in the hope of preventing him from saturating his nostalgia before she could prise anything useful from him. She found him sitting on the sofa, sober, much to her relief, and spruce in his habitual dress uniform. There was a piece of paper and a pen before him on the coffee table and neither glass nor bottle in sight.

'What have you got there?' she asked, peering with casual interest at the markings on the paper, 'some special boys' crossword?'

'My daily coded message,' he said, 'here, I'll show you how it works, if you like.'

Hildegard could hardly believe what she was hearing. Her heart began to pound and her mouth felt dry. In the end, she had needed to do nothing other than persevere, and now he would share his secrets of his own volition. After all these weeks, it was patience that had brought her to this moment. The relief bubbled both laughter and tears inside her, but the task was not yet complete, she must remain focussed. She perched as nonchalantly as she could manage on the arm of the sofa and watched intently over his shoulder as he explained the full workings of his cipher to her.

'Gosh, that's clever!' she said brightly as the chef appeared with a steaming dish for the table. 'I must just powder my nose before dinner.'

'Of course. Along the corridor to the left,' he folded the paper carefully into a leather document pouch and placed it on the low table.

Several hours later, Hildegard happily followed Mac through the little house to where Sir was waiting.

'Good evening, Hildegard, do make yourself comfortable. How was dinner this evening?'

'I have to say, I think it went rather well, Sir,' she could barely suppress a smile.

'How interesting,' he said, his eyes shining behind the thick lenses of his glasses. Hildegard seemed unusually excited to share the events of her evening, and he did so enjoy a story. 'Do tell.'

'Well, I arrived there a little ahead of time,' she began and then told him about the crossword cipher and how Urlateanu had shown her its key. Sir's face was suddenly serious.

'Good Lord. How much do you think you can remember? I'll have Mac bring some paper, we must get this down immediately.'

'No need,' she said. She reached into her handbag and brought out her green enamelled compact, which popped easily open. She placed it on the side table, carefully removed the velvet puff and powder well and took out the folded piece of toilet paper concealed underneath. Opening it out delicately she said 'I went straight to the bathroom and wrote it all down. I even left a powder smudge on my face so he would think I had actually been powdering my nose. Here, I'm sure it's right.'

He took the paper from her and held it between them, studying the pencil marks as she explained to him their meaning. She bit her lip while he silently traced his finger over the marks, committing the system to his memory, just as she had done herself a few hours earlier.

'Incredible,' he said under his breath. Then looking at her, 'This is very important Hildegard, having the code key could save weeks, even months of work on this. Well done.'

'Thank you, Sir,' Hildegard allowed herself a smile. She had always hoped that she could be of some small use, but this felt like something significant, something worthwhile.

'With this and the intercepted messages, we will be able to find out exactly what our Rumanian friend is up to. Are there any more dinners planned?'

'Yes, in a couple of weeks. I'll try to get him talking a bit about it, now that he has shown me that. I didn't want to seem too interested this evening and make him suspicious.'

'Good. But do remember, if you are caught, we know nothing about you.' Hildegard thought she detected a trace of regret, or perhaps apology in his voice as he gave his usual warning.

Chapter 38

A week into November Sam came back from Bucharest for a few days. Hildegard was delighted to see him, but quickly sensed that he was restless. When she mentioned it, he told her that he had decided he needed a change and had applied to work for the New York Times. He was hopeful of finishing for the Chicago Tribune soon, and starting his new job in the new year.

'What about your "part-time" work? Will you be able to continue with that?' Hildegard asked.

'Yes, the Times is behind the OSS, and the SOE by association, that won't be a problem.'

'So where do you think you will be, then? Will you stay in Bucharest?'

'I don't know yet, nothing has been confirmed. Maybe the Balkans or somewhere in Europe, maybe further into the Middle East. I miss being where the action is.' He was sitting on the floor in his old apartment which she had moved into during the summer's repatriation purge, Mr Mouse was lying next to him, his head on Sam's lap, black eyes gazing adoringly up at his friend. Hildegard stood facing away from them, looking out of the window. She did not turn around.

'Don't worry, H,' said Sam gently, 'you'll be the first to know, just as soon as I do.'

'It's alright,' she said, turning to look at him, really look at him. His face was so familiar to her now. She knew the concern writ there was genuine, he was worried for her. She knew such a vulnerable emotion would never be betrayed in public, where he was approachable, easy-going Sam, everybody's friend. She knew too that he was trying to hide another emotion from her now, his excitement at going back into the fray.

'I think I knew you'd had enough of second-hand news in the summer when Chas came back. You have been to so many places and seen so many things, you are never going to be happy tied to one place for too long, are you? You will always want to go and see for yourself what is happening in the world.'

'I guess so,' he agreed, smiling sheepishly, 'and what about you? Who knows how long the war will go on for, but when it's over, will you go back to Germany and find Eleanor?'

'Yes. Of course. But I won't live there again, I think it will be some time before I can forgive Germany. Maybe never. I want my future to be in England, if they'll have me.'

Sam nodded, absentmindedly scratching Mouse's head, still resting in his lap.

'I'd like to know you're OK, H,' he said eventually. 'My sister would tell you I'm a pretty lousy correspondent, but for the people that matter I do my best. And that does include her. And you.'

Hildegard had thought it would be awful to say a final farewell to Sam, but as the moment arrived, she felt at peace with the situation. The path she wanted to follow was becoming clear to her. It was not necessarily easy, but it was straightforward. As soon as she could, she would make her way to England, find Eleanor, and bring her over to a new home and a new life. She would get a job to support them both and be a proper mother to her daughter. That would be the hardest part, she had no doubt, but she would try, she would try her very best, because for everything that had happened, none of it was Eleanor's fault.

But Sam's path was different, he had spent years meandering around the globe. From Yale he had gone to the Sorbonne, to India, the Middle East, North Africa, and back to Europe. He did not know where he would go next, but he was ready to travel. His journalism gave him a constant supply of new places, new people, new events, and he thrived on it. He loved the excitement of it all, and the secret part-time work he undertook alongside the writing only added to the experience for him. For a while, their paths had run parallel, and she was glad that they had, but now they had reached the point of divergence, and that was alright too

Chapter 39

A day or two after Sam had returned to Rumania, Hildegard took the ferry across the Golden Horn and spent a couple of enjoyable hours wandering the labyrinthine alleys of the Grand Bazar. She lost all track of time in the ancient market, with its noise and its bustle, its beautiful, vaulted ceilings and the stones worn smooth underfoot by a millenia of customers gone before. Every trader vied for business, loudly showing off their vibrant wares of silks and ceramics, oils and spices, soft leathers and kilims, as the fleet-footed coffee sellers wove improbably quickly between the crowds. It was the most intense concentration of everything exotic imaginable and Hildegard loved it. Eventually she found herself in the very heart of the bazaar, where the silversmiths and traders congregated, and there also found what she was looking for.

The next dinner with Scarlat Urlateanu was looming, and with Christmas not far away, she thought it appropriate to take a gift this time. She bought an Ottoman dagger, a little larger than a paperknife and razor sharp. It was old, and beautifully crafted, with intricate swirled silverwork to the grip and guard, which she thought would appeal to Scarlat. The dagger was for sale at a good price that included a richly embroidered velvet scabbard that replaced it's lost silver original. The vendor balanced the knife across his forefinger to demonstrate it's perfect weighting, and she hoped the quality of the piece would speak for itself.

Scarlat was delighted with the dagger when she presented it to him, and spent several minutes admiring it, turning it over again and again. It's fine elegance became fragile at the mercy of his paw-like hands. In return, he gave Hildegard a small, oval-faced gold ladies' watch on a burgundy leather strap.
'It was intended for my fiancée in Vienna, but who knows when I shall see her again. You must wear it instead. Wear it always,' he insisted.
'Thank you, it's beautiful,' she said, putting it on.
The evening had begun well, and Scarlat was calmer and more amiable than Hildegard had seen him. After the main course was served, and the gap-toothed servant had retreated, Scarlat cleared his throat.
'My dear, we have met several times now. I find you to be a sympathetic listener and I do feel that I can trust you. There are a few things I would like to tell you.' He looked directly at her to convey his sincerity. 'You know now about my love for my nation, and my political views, and since the last time we met, you also know about my wireless communications. I would like to share with you some more details of my work here, the missions that I have.'
'All right,' said Hildegard. This was it. Her heart was pounding and she was completely focussed, but with many months of practice now, seamlessly maintained her composure. Anna would have been proud.
'You have more than one?' she asked, as though enquiring after his children.
'Indeed I do. One which I have been given, and one that I have devised myself.'
'I see.'
'The one I was given came from Berlin, a Dr Schuback. He is in charge of the office communicating with German intelligence

officers here, Herr Wolff, for example. I do not think you know Dr Schuback?'

She shook her head.

'It is Schuback whom I am sending wireless transmissions. Since the break in diplomatic relations between Turkey and the Axis, and the incarceration of the German legation to Istanbul, Berlin has fewer sources of information here. That is my first function. Then, as you know, the Nazis are rather on the back foot in the war now, and certain of them are making plans in case they do not recover and the worst happens in the future. They want to establish a series of small nests of sleeping agents provocateurs, a fifth column, to stay behind in Turkey and assist a Nazi resurrection when the time is right. A Mob organisation, they call it.'

Hildegard was noting every detail in order to pass it all on to Sir later.

'In fact,' he leaned toward her conspiratorially, 'they have even a Sixth Column. That is Gestapo men, believed to be dead, but actually living under false identities across the Balkans, waiting to lead the Nazi resurgence. Nobody knows about them, it is top secret, as the Americans would say. But I think you can be trusted,' he said again, then leaned back in his chair.

'Somewhat conveniently, the solution to the disarray in my own country, in my view, lies in a nationalist resurgence of a similar nature there. My intention is to extend Schuback's mission, and personally build a fifth column within and for Rumania, which will simultaneously act when the fascist uprising begins elsewhere, so that, God willing, and with the guidance of the souls of our ancestors, nationalism will be restored. Then the green shirts of the Iron Guard can once again be worn with pride, and Rumania will rightfully be restored for the Rumanians alone.'

He paused to wallow in his own melodrama, clearly overcome by the emotion behind his plan. Hildegard felt her stomach turn.

'Of course, there is some natural justice here as well. I believe a debt is owed by the Nazis. For years they supported the Iron Guard, they thought to use us as a convenient fifth column within Rumania. But they turned their backs on us, and what did we do to deserve that? Exactly as the Nazis do themselves, rid ourselves of the immigrant threat.'

Scarlat's indignation at this hypocrisy was clear. The Iron Guard had indeed been supported by the Nazis as he described. When the Germans had first arrived in Rumania, the Legion's new leader, Horia Sima, joined Antonescu in the senior ranks of government. He formed a self-regulating Legionary Police force, who embarked upon a murderous, merciless governance. As Prime Minister, Antonescu had had to assert his authority, the Iron Guard's unchecked terrorist rampage undermined him and also risked provoking German interference in his rule. He punished the Legion for their violence, by officially disbanding them. Hitler weighed in on Antonescu's side, threatening to withdraw his support for the Iron Guard in favour of the government. But the Legion would not be quieted. There were rumours of plans for an ambitious revolution and the seizing of power from Antonescu. The Iron Guard had lost their founding father, and without Codreanu's ideological guidance, they had followed the extremely violent Sima down a steep descent into anarchy. There were gun fights in the streets, prompting a heavy-handed response from the government, still backed by Hitler, to end the Legionary revolt.

In January 1941, the Iron Guard began the most sadistic of pogroms against the Jews. Hundreds of people were murdered or mutilated, and their property destroyed. The slaughter was eventually halted by the army, sent in by Antonescu to quell the violence, with German army reinforcements. This was the ultimate betrayal for the Iron Guard, that their fascist brothers would prevent them annihilating Jews. They had admired Hitler, but any reciprocation of that admiration had been too easily abandoned. Hitler needed stability in Rumania, both as a stepping-stone for his territorial ambitions to the east and for the all-important oil supply to remain uninterrupted. He considered Antonescu's government the more reliable option in Rumania and as an independent entity with no external support, the Iron Guard collapsed.

After that, the Legion continued only in a ceremonial role, their distinctive green shirts worn solely for official occasions. Scarlat had disingenuously chosen not to share the excesses of the Iron Guards violence with Hildegard. He had edited it out of their past and future histories.

'You understand the imperative here? I must restore the Rumanian nation, and the Legion at all costs.'

Hildegard nodded, 'Of course.'

In a heartbeat, the fine, cold blade of the dagger was at her throat. Time stopped for Hildegard, she did not breathe. She looked into Scarlat's eyes and saw that his soul belonged to the Iron Guard.

'If you betray me now, or indeed ever, I will have no hesitation in killing you with this very weapon,' he hissed.

She felt the pressure of the blade against her neck and in that still, infinite moment, believed him. Another heartbeat and the dagger was back in its scabbard. A silent stream of air escaped from her lungs.

The servant carried a rattling tray in from the kitchen.

'Ah! Dessert,' said Scarlat pleasantly.

Chapter 40

Sir looked at the ceiling and exhaled softly.

'I'm sorry, Hildegard, that must have been very frightening.'

'I'm not afraid of him, but I am afraid of what he is capable of doing. And not just the knife. I am well aware what extremes political fanatics will go to in the name of their cause. What he told me of his plans made my blood run cold. I just want to stop him.'

'Of course. And you are right. The sixth column does sound like a particularly sinister hydra. It'll take a truly Herculean effort to cauterise that one. Interesting that it has a lair outside of Germany, you would expect them to defend the fatherland to the last, but to scatter cells all over the Balkans is either very ambitious or very desperate. But forewarned is forearmed.'

'He wants to manipulate it all for his own purpose. He thinks he can piggy-back his own personal revolution on a future Nazi resurgence. His support for the Germans is based purely on self-interest. I'm not even sure he has any support at home.'

'I told you he was a rogue agent. He has a reputation as a diabolical double-crosser, and I can see why. Well, he's certainly in the right place for such byzantine scheming.' Sir smiled sympathetically at Hildegard and poured them both more brandy. She was beginning to feel a little better now, cradled in the warmth of the welcoming fire in this familiar place, and the silken ribbons of the music from the gramophone. She sipped her brandy gratefully.

'Apparently Wolff has been asking about you in Therapia,' said Sir, as though the interned Gestapo were a close mutual friend.

'Really? I was hoping I'd seen the last of him. What did he want?'

'News. I didn't want him to think you've been slacking, so I sent Ferruh back with a report from you. It seems that you have heard that the new British ambassador has offered conditions to Turkey to become a recognised Allied state. Along the lines that they loosen their home policy, allow equal rights for minorities, remove the ban on political parties and allow free elections, that sort of thing.'

'I am well informed, aren't I?' said Hildegard.

'Oh, that's not all. If you're interested, you also said that the Ambassador thinks Turkey should look to the Middle East rather than Europe for its economic development at present and they should dismiss all their anti-Allied diplomats and officials. What else?' he asked himself, 'Oh yes, you said he wants the straits opened up for the free passage of shipping, and is offering inclusion in the United Nations Relief and Rehabilitation Administration, in return.'

'I haven't been slacking at all then. Thank you, Sir,' she said with a smile.

'Of course, you also said that Turkey have declined the offer at present, but it will still have rattled Wolff that Allied diplomatic pressure is being applied to Turkey and there's nothing he can do about it. It doesn't hurt to lower camp morale,' said Sir. 'It's already low, there's still no sign of them going home. We'll leave him to stew in that, I think. Now then, when is your meeting with Ludwig?'

'The day after tomorrow. They're letting me in to the Consulate because of my German papers, but Ferruh assures me the police won't cause me any problems as I am also British.'

'I think you can trust Ferruh on that,' said Sir. 'But not Ludwig, treat him with caution. The impression I have is that he is potentially dangerous, he has a lot of connections still at large in the city and he is able to maintain fairly good communications with them. See what he wants but be careful.'

'Yes Sir.'

'And again, it is my duty to remind you that if you are caught, we know nothing about you.'

Chapter 41

Two days later the armed Turkish police guard allowed Hildegard to enter the German Consulate building for her appointment with Thomas Ludwig which Ferruh had set up. She had not met Ludwig before but Sir had provided her with information about him, which he had obtained from the same defectors about whom Sam had reported on the day he brought Mouse to Hildegard.

Ludwig was a member of the German intelligence community in Istanbul, but he had not joined the RSHA like Wolff. In fact, he regarded the Gestapo and their brethren with some disdain, as an organisation of unprincipled murderers. He had chosen instead to work for the Abwehr, the military intelligence organisation whose leader, Admiral Canaris, he considered a man of conscience.

Before the war, Ludwig had made a living trading carpets but always fancied himself something of an artist. On signing up, it had been made clear to him that it was unacceptable for Germany to be represented abroad by a person with a Jewish name, so Thomas Levin had readily become Thomas Ludwig. He adopted his new profession with the same chameleon ease as he adopted his new identity.

Ludwig's office was in a different part of the consulate to Wolff's, in a building below the main one in the grounds, off the same steep road where Hildegard used to live. She entered warily and was greeted by a tall, thin man with receding grey hair and an inscrutable expression.

'Cigarette?' he opened the box on his desk and offered it to her.

'No, thank you.'

'You don't believe the rumours about me, do you?'

'Rumours?' she said.

'I'm considered a dangerous man,' he told her with no humour but more than a little pride. 'Apparently I keep a supply of lethal potions and poisoned cigarettes here. And I ruthlessly dispatch anyone who offends me directly into the Bosphorus through a trap door in the floor.'

'I see,' said Hildegard evenly, she had not yet worked him out. 'I hadn't heard that, no.'

'It's all nonsense, of course, mere propaganda. Would you like to check, under the carpet? See if there's a rill flowing beneath the floor, that would sweep you out to sea?' Hildegard shook her head.

'The Turkish police do not generally turn a blind eye to dead bodies found floating in the channel,' he went on, 'Still, it amuses me to frighten the junior members of the legation. They call this office Ludwigshaven and avoid coming here at all costs. It suits me perfectly.'

Hildegard smiled politely but her little amber cigarette holder remained in her handbag, just in case.

'To business.' he went on. 'Ferruh tells me you have done some good work for Wolff.'

'Do you work with Wolff?' she asked.

'No. In theory I work for him, but I know far more about what he does than he knows about me.'

The spate of defections at the beginning of the year in Istanbul had been the final nail in the coffin for the entire Abwehr network. Already suspicious of the organisation, Hitler had sacked Canaris in fury at the betrayals in Turkey and handed over the functions of the Abwehr to the RSHA, under Walter Schellenberg. In effect, Abwehr officers were now subordinate to the Sicherheitsdeinst, although in Istanbul, there was no practical evidence of this restructure.

'Yes, I know far more about a lot of things than he does,' Ludwig went on. 'I have my own sources, of course, but I see all reports submitted to this consulate for Wolff, and everyone else's as well. I would say I am the best informed intelligence officer here, even now.'

Ludwig boasted with some justification, he really was well informed. His incarceration in the Consular complex, although inconvenient, had not prevented him from running his many agents in the city, just as he had always done. He gathered information on the intelligence services of all nations represented there, spying on the spies.

He had also contrived to be passed every intelligence report that entered the German Consulate, regardless of its intended recipient. Russia was uniquely excluded from his wide-cast net because of Turkish sensitivity to the Soviet threat. Any person known to have a connection with them, even by running an agent against them, was automatically under the host nation's suspicion.

And nothing escaped the sharp observation of the Turkish intelligence service, Ludwig knew that. Russian issues aside, he prided himself on being the best informed German intelligence officer in Istanbul. Hildegard tried her best to look impressed, despite her already high level of acute anxiety being elevated further by his cold, sinister smile. She was relieved that she herself had never submitted a written report to Wolff.

'What is it you wanted to see me about?' she had no wish to extend this interview longer than necessary.

'As I said, I know you have worked for Bruno Wolff. I also know you have a connection with the Rumanians, the Vice Consul, who in turn has a connection with Berlin. I understand they plan to continue that connection after we have left. We, the military intelligence that is, are putting our own stay-behind organisation in place. We are all expecting to be returned to Germany imminently, as you know and it is imperative that communications with Turkey continue after we have gone. As you are reported to provide reliable information, I would like you to collude with Ferruh in this important work.'

Chapter 42

'That was interesting,' Hildegard told Sir later. 'He seems convinced I'm genuine. I told him, like you said, that I was waiting for a Swiss man to bring me a passport so that I can leave too, but that he hasn't turned up yet. Ludwig didn't seem to think there was much he would be able to do to help me, although he did say rather half-heartedly that he would try. It didn't sound like there was any active communication between the German Consulate and the Swiss anyway. But he was more interested in his own plans for after they leave. It would suit him better if I stay here.'

'And what are his plans?'

'He's trying to set up a fifth column cell. They seem to be all the rage at the moment. The consular staff are all still waiting to be shipped back to Germany, but he wants to maintain radio contact with a stay-behind cell and receive information from them. Or us, I should say.'

'Us?'

'Ferruh and me. He asked if I would work with them,' Hildegard sighed, 'I know Ferruh will do anything to keep the Russians out of Turkey, but it's a bit different for me.'

Hildegard had grave misgivings about Ludwig's proposal.

'What is it that troubles you about it? You have been convincingly loyal to them this past year, why not carry on? It could be useful to us.'

'I know it could. But what if Turkey does declare for the Allies? Everyone says they will, and you tell me I've even sent Wolff a report on the negotiations. If that does actually happen, then the whole thing becomes doubly dangerous, not to mention unpalatable, for me. I'd be actively working for the enemy against an Allied nation, from within that nation. With no safety net,' she said grimly.

The fifths and sixth columns described by Scarlat were the creation of the Gestapo and the Sicherheistdeinst. Scarlat had received his orders directly from Schuback in Berlin, and the scheme was known to Wolff, although according to Ferruh he was not directly involved and appeared dismissive of it. Whether Wolff had genuine doubts about the value of the plan or whether, after the farce with the American wireless set in Sofia and the whole sorry saga with Miss Goldacker, he just still distrusted Urlateanu, they did not know. Ferruh was of the opinion that Wolff distrusted everybody, and he played down the fifth column scheme as a way of proving his own loyalty to the Fuhrer and at the same time hoping his scepticism would detract from the obvious importance of the plan.

It was true that such plans had to be implemented with extreme caution. The Fuhrer considered them defeatist and mercilessly punished as traitors those found to be involved. But the Gestapo was not the only organisation making plans in case of defeat. The Abwehr was also setting up stay-behind cells of agents. It was in one of these that Ludwig wanted Hildegard to participate, alongside Ferruh.

'You're right, of course,' said Sir carefully. After all she had done already, he would not put pressure on her to take that next step. 'It's entirely your decision, if you are to be recruited by him.'

'I'm not sure if I can,' she said after a moment. 'I do understand it would be useful, to be a set of eyes and ears for you, but really, it's asking a lot. It's different for Ferruh. Turkey is still concerned about the Russian advance, so he would just be safeguarding his country, presumably with their backing. But for me, it's just very dangerous, and I don't honestly know if the risk would be worth it, what really is to be gained from it.'

The situation she would potentially put herself in was crystal clear to Hildegard. She understood too that she had a choice. Suddenly she felt exhausted, too tired even to cry.

'Everyone is saying that the war will be over soon anyway, and I just want to go home. To England.'

She stared bleakly ahead as Sir spoke again.

'Hildegard, I think it's only fair to tell you, this will be our last meeting.' Hildegard closed her eyes, her decision was made. She had struggled to justify continuing to place herself in the dangerous position that liaising with Scarlat, Wolff, Ludwig and even Ferruh had put her. Each of them had presented a threat to her in some way. The one person in all of this whose respect she valued, who might have persuaded her simply by not attempting to coerce her, was Sir. She might have done it for him, but he was leaving.

'I'll be moving on from here very soon. We're having a bit of a reorganisation, but I cannot tell you any more than that. It remains my duty to inform you that should you be caught...'

'I know, Sir, I know,' Hildegard interrupted him. She could not bear to hear those words tonight. 'Just this once, please tell London that I release you from your obligation to inform me of my status.'

They sat in silence for some time, watching the flames. She, contemplating an unknown future and he, feeling what? Not guilt exactly, but a degree of responsibility for her. London had always been clear on their position on most issues, the importance of keeping agents' identities secret, of maintaining deniability wherever possible. These things he had done.

Hildegard had publicly remained that German woman from Taksim's, however misleading a truth that was. He had dutifully reported his intelligence to Cairo, and never identified his sources to his colleagues there either. She was still undeniably deniable.

But London had also been clear on their view of other intelligence organisations, specifically the Americans, who had arrived in Istanbul not many months before Hildegard, ready and eager to participate in the secret war.

London considered them very much the new boys and the junior partners, even something of a liability with their lack of experience, and certainly not serious contributors to the cause. He knew they did not always receive a full and timely briefing, or any briefing at all in certain circumstances, such was London's disregard for them. What he had done was entirely justified, he told himself, by London's stance. He took his orders from them after all. But now he was not sure that his actions had been right, not sure at all. He had no problem with the Americans themselves, he quite liked some of them, although he despaired sometimes that their public behaviour was rather too public for their profession, and he could quite see London's concerns over that. But had he been right? London certainly considered them of little significance, dispensable even, and he had not given Hildegard all of their names, just a few, to pass on to Wolff. That had been her very first task, and she had not questioned it, beyond a mild "But they're our friends, aren't they Sir?"

He had assured her that no harm would come of it, and it was of paramount importance that she gained Wolff's confidence. Information of this calibre would secure his trust. And so it had, just as he had predicted, and she had gone on to prove herself time and time again.

He almost convinced himself that he had taken a risk and it had paid off. But as he stared into the flames, he examined his own conscience and knew, if he was honest with himself, that the risk had been Hildegard's alone. If the Americans had discovered what she had done, on his orders, he would have had to abandon her, disclaim responsibility and cut all connection with her. She would have been rendered useless as an agent for Wolff too, and he would have sent her back to Germany and who knew what fate. She had known all of this, right from the start, and she had accepted the risk. At best, she would be labelled as a double agent, whom either side would neither claim nor rescue. But that implied a mercenary ambivalence that he knew she did not possess. There was no uncertainty about Hildegard Reilly's commitment, and nothing but uncertainty about her future. Now she faced being left behind alone.

The fire was dying in the grate when they stood to shake hands.

'Goodbye, Sir.'

'Good luck, Hildegard. Goodbye.'

Chapter 43

Since the German diplomatic legation had been interned on 2nd September, they had been waiting to go home. The original plan at the time of the diplomatic break with Turkey had been for an exchange of diplomats from both nations to take place in the Balkans. However, the rapid advance of the Red Army following the capitulation of Rumania meant the Balkan exchange was impossible and so the services of the SS Drottningholm were sought instead.

In peaceful times, the Drottningholm was an ocean liner, employed in transporting passengers between Sweden and New York. During the war, the civilian crew bravely agreed to provide repatriation services for nations on both sides of the conflict, protected only by a coat of white paint and the messages daubed on either flank that this was a neutral vessel with diplomats aboard, reinforced by large Swedish flags painted between the lettering. At sea, the ship was lit from bow to stern, and sailed in the hope that these measures would be enough to stay the aim of any torpedo gunner, leaving only the threats of a mistaken aerial attack and the precarious navigation of the sea mines. By Christmas 1944, the Drottningholm had yet to appear in Istanbul.

Since September, those Germans that remained had been divided into groups and distributed across several locations. In Istanbul, some were in the German School, some the former Austrian Embassy, and some, including Ludwig, in the German Consulate. Wolff was among those despatched to the embassy summer residence a short distance north along the coast at Therapia.

Ferruh had been made the buyer for the Therapia camp, responsible for providing essential supplies, but also supervising and controlling conditions in the camp on behalf of the Turkish intelligence service. The break in diplomatic links did not rule out continued unofficial communications and the day before the internments, Wolff had furnished Ferruh with a radio set robust enough to maintain contact directly with Berlin, essential now that the relay radio station previously used in Bucharest had been destroyed.

Wolff had ventured to suggest, in the vaguest of terms, the possibility of Turkey's brokering a peace between Germany and the Western Allies, without Russian involvement, which he believed would also be to Turkey's advantage. Ferruh had returned with the Turkish response that while they agreed that such an outcome would be favourable, they saw no possibility of the eastern front being pushed back by the German army under such circumstances and so declined his offer. In the months since, while the German military situation had gone from dire to catastrophic, Ferruh had been exchanging messages with Berlin on Wolff's behalf, with the approval of both sides.

Wolff was careful to maintain good relations with Ferruh, who was his only link with the outside world. He had no contact with his colleagues in the other internment camps, so apart from Ferruh, he was isolated.

Ludwig, on the other hand, had direct access to a functional radio set in the consulate building and had been able to maintain an erratic contact with Berlin, via a relay station in Vienna. He reported the work he had done to establish a fifth column cell for when the last of the German colony eventually left Istanbul. He would be depending on Ferruh and Reilly to supply reliable information to the legation, after they had left.

Hildegard declined another dinner invitation from Scarlat in the new year, claiming ill health. She was only sick, however, of the war, which ground incessantly on. Sam had been in Cairo since Christmas, ready to start work for the New York Times, and Sir had now also left Istanbul. It was time for her to start thinking about leaving too.

The early morning walks had become a new habit, and were often now quite long, despite the cold. Mr Mouse relished the freedom, running wherever an interesting sight or scent lead him. For Hildegard the dawn light was both calming and inspiring, like a meditation. This morning they reached the park at the top of a hill, their breath rising in clouds as they climbed the last steep path through an avenue of stark, stripped trees, their jagged spiky fingers appealing hopelessly to an indifferent heaven. It was worth the effort. Beneath the trees, there was a bench where Hildegard liked to sit and hear the early call to prayer coax the timid winter sun above the rolling hills on the opposite shore. At this time of year, the Bosphorus made its eternal way south with a grim, steely determination that was irreconcilable with the blithe blue waters of summertime. She watched as the sunlight strengthened enough to dispel the mist on the surface, and she imagined the whorls and swirls of the currents too far away to see and thought of Sam.
A man sat down beside her, dewdrops glistened on the polished toes of his shoes, and Hildegard noticed the dampness on the turned-up hems of his sharply creased trousers. He reached into

the inside pocket of his impeccably cut overcoat and handed her a thick envelope.

'From Wolff,' he said. 'He still believes you are genuine and feels obliged to help you.'

Hildegard put the envelope in her pocket without opening it. She knew it would contain money but she had settled her moral dilemma about such payments long ago.

'They're still there, then, in Therapia?' she asked.

'Yes, there's no sign of the ship yet. But there is some news,' he paused, 'As of yesterday, there will be no more messages from Wolff on my radio set to Berlin. It has suddenly stopped working. On the orders of the Turkish intelligence service.'

'Really? Did they tell you why?'

'No. But I can only assume it indicates a national step closer to the Allies.'

Hildegard turned to him.

'You think Turkey will finally enter the war against Germany, Ferruh?'

'It seems likely, wouldn't you say?'

'Yes, I suppose it does,' said Hildegard tentatively, hope and fear sparring for her attention. She and Ferruh sat in separate silences for a while, then both spoke at once.

'It puts you in a difficult position.'

'Will you carry on working for them?'

'For me, it is simpler,' said Ferruh. 'I am not alone, as you are and if I continue, it is with the agreement of my country, to make absolutely certain of protection from the Russians. The enemy of my enemy is my friend, as they say. Yes, I will continue for Ludwig, here in Istanbul, but not for the Gestapo, not Wolff. I will only act as buyer for the camp at Therapia now, not messenger.'

'Ludwig also thinks I am genuine. He thinks I will work with you for him, even after they leave. Especially after they leave,' Hildegard said.

'He can continue to think that.' Ferruh turned toward her. 'Look, I know people think I am mercenary, but I am loyal to Turkey and while we have been carefully sitting on the fence in this war,

I have done all I can to maintain good relations on both sides, in my country's best interests. Until now, it has never been certain which way we might eventually need to jump. I have done what I have had to do and I make no apology for that. I will assure Ludwig of your continued commitment to his cause, then there will be no interference for you from any of his many friends in this city. But the Turks will know that you are on the side of the Allies.'

'Thank you, Ferruh. I appreciate your doing this, you don't owe me anything.'

Ferruh turned to look at her and after a moment's consideration, spoke kindly.

'I think we are the same, you and I. Both doing what has to be done for our countries. Difficult and dangerous things, yes, but necessary. And it looks as though we will shortly be officially on the same side. I am happy to help you, Hildegard.'

Hildegard sighed. Ferruh had proved himself a friend and his words brought some comfort, but there were other problems still unresolved.

'Now I just have the persistent Rumanian to worry about.'

'I don't think you need concern yourself with him anymore.'

'Why not?'

'I gather he is effectively redundant, now that his contact in Berlin has been removed from his post.'

'Schuback?'

'Yes. His fifth column plans were discovered by his superiors, and they don't take kindly to what they see as defeatist activities.'

'So Scarlat has lost his Nazi support, just like the rest of the Iron Guard. I don't imagine that has affected his position any, nor will stop his scheming. It's probably made him more determined than ever. But at least he's on his own now.'

Ferruh nodded slowly. 'And what will you do now?'

'Everything I can to get back to England, Ferruh.'

She left Ferruh on the bench and walked briskly back down the tree lined path with Mr Mouse trotting at her heel.

Chapter 44

Istanbul, February 1945

Three weeks into February 1945, Turkey declared to join the hostilities against Germany. By then, Hildegard was desperate to leave. There was nothing left for her in Istanbul. She had worked most diligently, most carefully, most secretly for the British for over a year and now that Turkey was no longer neutral, she was at risk of being exposed as a German spy, a role she had never undertaken. But that was not the worst of her troubles.

She was extremely worried for Eleanor and Anna in Silesia. The Red Army was advancing west in a broad sweep with devastating speed and aggression, and the border mountains were directly in its path. She had managed to send them a parcel which might be of some use or value, if it had reached them in time, or even at all. There was no certainty of that, with the border inevitably closed after the Turkish declaration, and in any case it was a small contribution that did little to allay her fears for them.

'Have you heard from Sam?' said Peter, settling into his seat. They had arranged to meet for a drink in the Snake Pit, the bar in the Park Hotel.

'Yes, I had a letter. He's enjoying Cairo and getting on well for the New York Times,' she said. 'What about you? Any news from home?' she was almost afraid to ask.

'No, nothing direct since the Russians took Belgrade. We are, what is it you say, out of the frying pan and into the fire?'

'I fear you are right, Peter. The Red Army seems to be thundering west unstoppably. I hope your family are safe.'

'Yours too, they are also in the way of the Soviets, no?'

They sat quietly, in helpless communion, both of their families under threat from a new direction, neither of them able to do anything about it.

'One day, this will all be over, and we can begin our lives again, find our families, follow our dreams.'

'I hope so, Peter,' Hildegard sighed. 'What will you do when the war is over? Stay here to finish your studies, or go back to Belgrade?'

'Neither,' he said, 'I plan to go to America. The land of the free! I want to study there, and maybe teach in one of the great universities. That's my dream.'

Hildegard smiled at her friend, always the optimist.

'That's a good dream, and they'd be lucky to have you. I hope you make it there. You can write to me in England.'

'Of course!' he raised his glass for a toast, 'To dreams.'

'To dreams.'

With no purpose to her remaining in Turkey, Hildegard devoted her energy to finding a way to return to England. She tried first at the British Consulate and was dismayed to find that judging by the crowd in the foyer, most of the rest of the British people in Istanbul were doing the same.

'I'm sorry, Miss, but there are no passages on board ship available,' the clerk told her when she eventually reached the desk.

'But this is the consulate, can't you do anything to help a British subject repatriate? Here, my passport.' She showed the man the paper that proved her Britishness, but he shook his head.

'I'm sorry, Miss,' he said again, 'but as you can see, the world and his wife wants to go home now. I'm afraid there's rather a long queue ahead of you.'

Diplomatic staff and their families had priority for the few tickets that did become available, but even for them it was difficult to secure passage.

'What about Mac?' she had asked in desperation, maybe he could help, 'Is there someone here by the name of MacPherson?'

'No, Miss, nobody here by that name,' the clerk had told her patiently. He had spoken kindly to her, but there was nothing within his gift to give her. She thanked him and turned away, putting her precious passport carefully back in her bag.

Day after day she walked miles around the city, visiting every point of departure she could think of, the port, the railway station, even the airstrip, but every way she turned, the route was blocked. The answer was always the same, there were no tickets available on any form of transport, to anywhere.

After yet another dispiriting day, Hildegard could not face returning to an empty apartment, and found herself meandering up to Sultanahmet and into the Blue Mosque. It was not yet prayer time and with her head covered, she joined the shoeless faithful milling around inside. The mosque's interior was luminous even on such a grey day, but Hildegard did not notice. Lattice wooden screens demarcated the women's section to one side, and she wandered in. She found a space and sat in solitude, grateful for the sanctuary offered. Around her, other women sat alone, lost in private prayers, or talking quietly in groups on the carpet. Small children ran between them, chasing each other, playing happily. The women's section cradled a tranquil sisterhood of friends and families. It was a place of love, a place of peace. Hildegard bowed her head and covered her face with her hands to hide the sudden flood of tears that drenched her cheeks. She had never felt so lonely.

That evening, as every other, she returned home exhausted and demoralised.

'We'll find a way eventually, Mouse,' she said as he flopped on the floor beside her. But even saying the words aloud did not make them convincing. The truth was that she was stranded here, almost friendless, helpless and sick with worry for her family's unknown fate as the Red Army thundered on toward them.

Chapter 45

Kiesewald, Silesia February 1945

'The Russians are coming!' Hedda exploded into the kitchen in an agitated flurry of snowflakes. They all turned to look at her.

'It's true!' she said breathlessly, 'They're already at Breslau, that's only a hundred kilometres away. What are we going to do?'

Eleanor did not know any Russians, but from what she had heard the grown-ups say, she did not think their arrival would be a good thing.

'Do you know what they do to people?' Hedda looked at each of them, 'What they do to women?' her voice became a terrified whisper. She was wide-eyed but there was a seriousness in her expression that was not there when she pulled this face to tease

Eleanor. This time, the bold and daring Hedda was truly afraid and that in turn scared Eleanor. Maria and Anna exchanged a glance.

'They're saying we can leave now, it's alright for us to leave. Come on, we have to go!' Hedda insisted impatiently.

Until now, the civilians of Silesia had been forbidden to evacuate. Despite the Red Army advance, the Nazis had considered it a sign of capitulation and therefore a punishable offence for anyone to run.

'That's enough, Hedda. It doesn't help to panic. I think we should go down to see if we can get rail tickets out of here. Where to, I have no idea. Bring the suitcase, Anna, that might help you at least.'

The suitcase had miraculously arrived the day before, from Hildegard. It contained a large salami-type sausage, fat and heavy with a wrinkled white skin, tied with string at either end. Its savoury, peppery scent had tempted them, but Anna knew that however hungry they were, this was a valuable item to trade with and although she had not expected to use it quite so immediately, she was grateful for it.

When they arrived at the usually sleepy village station lower down the slope, they could barely move for the crush of people pushing and arguing in their desperation to get away.

'It's like when we left Berlin, Grandma,' said Eleanor, taking hold of Anna's hand. There was a hand-written notice saying that there would be a special train laid on that evening for people who wished to leave, advising that travel permits and tickets were available, and stating a disheartening, astronomical price.

'Well that's us out,' said Maria. 'There's no way we could afford those tickets, even if there were any left after this lot.'

Anna looked across the mass of people. A few she recognised as mountain residents, but most were refugees from further east, clutching scant possessions, already fleeing the Russian advance. Their faces showed the same horror she had seen in the refugees escaping the Hamburg bombing eighteen months before. Eleanor was right, their escape from this place was a terrible repetition of their arrival.

Anna had heard stories of the Russians' brutality and knew that it was too dangerous to stay, they must get away. She spotted the stationmaster across the crowd, stepping slyly sideways along the back wall, toward the door to his office. She tightened her hold of Eleanor's hand, and with a firm grip on the suitcase with the other hand, forced their way determinedly through the throng. They reached the door just behind the vanishing stationmaster and Anna thrust the suitcase forward, to prevent the door from closing. Before he realised what was happening, Anna and Eleanor were leaning against the now closed door in his office, Anna clutching the suitcase to her chest.

'Madam, you cannot come in here. The ticket office is open in the foyer.' The stationmaster stood behind his desk, his last defence against the rabble.

'I know, and there are a thousand people trying to buy a hundred available tickets.'

'Most of them do not have the money. If you can pay, there is a good chance you will get one. Kindly…' He waved his hand dismissively toward the foyer behind her. Anna was undeterred.

'Sir. A good chance is not enough. I need to be sure. I have a child to think of, do you see? And I don't have money, but I do have something I can pay with.'

'What do you mean?' the stationmaster said, narrowing his eyes. This was no time to be cautious. Anna had watched him sneak away from the melée outside, shirking his responsibility and abandoning his subordinates to the implacable crowd. She had a feeling he would not act on principle, and this was their only chance of escape. She lay the suitcase on the desk and opened it.

'This,' she said, 'In exchange for two tickets, for myself and the child, and travel permits.'

The stationmaster ran his greedy eyes over the contents of the case, he was almost salivating. He was not new to being offered bribes, neither was he averse to accepting them, as Anna had guessed. Such an offering as this, such rich, beautiful food, had not been seen for years. He would take it.

'Done.' he said.

'We'll wait here while you make the arrangements,' said Anna firmly, snapping the lid closed and keeping hold of the case.

There was no time for lengthy farewells to their friends on the mountain. Maria and her daughters had neither people nor places to run to, and no means of paying the price of the tickets in any case.

'Oh my dear, I can hardly bear to leave you all here,' said Anna, holding Maria's hands, worry etched on her face. 'What will happen to you?'

'Don't you worry about us,' Maria said, feigning cheerfulness, 'We'll be fine. They say they are going to evacuate us all anyway. We'll just have to wait and hope they do it before the Russians get here.'

Anna and Eleanor packed their few belongings in a single case, Eleanor now adding Herman's sleeping wooden cat to her doll and her precious Klarchen book that made up her possessions. It was a sad and regrettably hurried departure, but they wished each other well as bravely as they could. Who knew what would happen to any of them?

Chapter 46

Back at the station, all of the luggage was loaded into an enormous snow scoop attached to the front of the engine, in order that as many people as possible could fit inside the carriages. The laden train chugged resolutely on, first west and then north. Eleanor pressed her nose against the window, watching the demolished country scroll slowly past. She saw a line of blackened ruins silhouetted against an orange glow in the distance.

'What is that, Grandma?'

'I think that was a town called Dresden,' said Anna bleakly.

They were dozing in their seats when the train stopped at the first of countless stations. Anna opened her eyes in time to see the disembarked passengers swarming around the snow plough on the engine.

'Stay here, Eleanor, do not move. I will be back very soon,' she instructed the sleepy and bewildered child before hurrying off the train. She was just in time to rescue their suitcase from the arms of a fellow traveller whose own case was lost, and who would thieve another in order to sell the contents in recompense.

On they trundled, the train lines and stations getting progressively worse with bomb damage, the further north into Germany they travelled. At every stop Anna would alight and stand near the snow plough in order to protect their belongings, which she had to defend more than once. They were getting used to the train stopping altogether and having to disembark and wait for hours on a cold platform, already crowded with other refugees and returning soldiers.

'Are your legs sore, Grandma?' asked Eleanor. Benches on the platforms were the prerogative of the soldiers, and while Eleanor could curl up on the suitcase, Anna's ankles were swollen from hours of standing.

'I'm all right,' said Anna, stoic as ever.

'Madam, please, take my seat,' a young man lifted his head to speak. He had been slumped on a bench next to them, his forearms on his knees and his head bowed with exhaustion. His boots were scuffed and his uniform looked as worn out as he did. Eleanor had thought he was asleep.

'Thank you, but I'm all right,' said Anna again.

'Really, I insist,' he said, standing and guiding her politely by the elbow.

'They'll shoot me if they see me taking your seat,' she said, only half joking.

'They'll shoot me first, for deserting,' he said with a wry and weary smile. Anna did not know what to say. He was one of so very many that they had seen along the journey, young men like him, boys, forced to go and fight, risking their lives whether they truly believed in the cause or just colluded in the pretence. Now that the cause was lost, there was no more pretence.

'I don't blame you,' said Anna, looking around at the dejected jumble of humanity scattered across the platform. 'What is there to fight for, anyway?' The young man looked at her with the improper sadness of his generation.

'You know, we were only ever fighting for each other,' he said quietly. 'All of us, brothers, looking out for each other, in it together. But we're not together now, so many are lost, and you're right, for what? I'm sick of it, I've just had enough of the whole pointless thing. I'm going home.'

Anna heard the echo of Herman's words about his loyalty to his friends in what this boy had said. She could only imagine the horrors they had witnessed, the friends who had become like family destroyed before them, escaping the same fate by providence alone. She was usually a stickler for any kind of rules, but she thought of the mothers, the sisters, the sweethearts and wives, and she did not blame the boys, this boy, for trying to get back to them. Somehow the rules did not seem to matter anymore. She wondered if Herman was doing the same.

'I hope you get home safely,' she told the young man, still thinking of her brother, 'and thank you for the seat.'

The next train clattered on toward the north, the stops and obstacles became increasingly frequent, and progress frustratingly slow. On the morning of the fourth day, the train drew to a halt at a place called Ennigerloh. Anna stroked Eleanor's hair and shook her shoulder gently.

'Wake up, Eleanor, we're going to get off here.'

'Are we home?' the little girl asked sleepily, lifting her head from her grandmother's lap to look out of the window.

'No, not quite, but I think we can stay here for a while. Come on, we've had enough of this train, haven't we?'

They retrieved their case from the snow plough and followed the straggle of tired travellers out of the station. Anna asked directions and they soon found themselves outside a house, whose door was opened by a woman of Anna's age.

'Mrs Brabender! What a surprise, we were not expecting...'

'Mrs Hermeier, please forgive me, I had no way of contacting you.'

'Come in, both of you, come in.'

Mr and Mrs Hermeier offered the most generous welcome they could, and listened while Anna relayed their tale of escape, and the exhausting train journey the entire length of the country, away from the mountains and the advancing Red Army.

'The further north we have travelled, the more difficult it has become. I wonder if we might be able to stay here a short while, I know it is not far to Neuss now, but we really cannot face any more travelling for the moment.'

'Of course,' said Mrs Hermeier. 'You are quite right, but I fear the last part of your journey will be even worse than you expect. Everything is bombed out, the roads, the bridges, the railways. After all the distance you have come so far, the last hundred and fifty kilometres look almost impossible for you, I'm sorry to tell you. But of course you must stay, we are happy to have you. You were so kind to little Inge last year, it is the least we can do.'

'Thank you, I am very grateful. It was a pleasure to have her,' said Anna with relief.

'Does Inge live here?' asked Eleanor hopefully.

'Not at the moment, but I think they may be trying to get here soon.' Mrs Hermeier turned to Anna, 'with the new baby, I think Agnes will find it impossible to stay in Bocholt. Their house is bomb damaged, and she has to use a ladder outside to go upstairs.' She shook her head, 'no, she will be much better off here, where we can help her, with all the girls so small still.'

Anna's sister Agnes was married to the Hermeier's son, Bernard, and Inge was their second child, then came Helga, and Ruth, whose birth had prompted Inge's stay with them in Silesia the previous year. Now there was to be a fifth baby, who would be another girl, Hilde.

'And what of Marianne? I heard she was taken into a special hospital to be cared for?' Anna was asking about the oldest daughter, who had learning difficulties.

'Oh, my dear, you have not heard? Poor Marianne! Agnes had a letter some weeks ago, from the sisters at the hospital, to say that Marianne had succumbed to disease, pneumonia, I believe it was. Apparently there was an outbreak among the patients which could not be controlled. It's very sad.'

The pain in Mrs Hermeier's voice at the death of her granddaughter was too raw to witness, and Anna turned her face away as her own heart broke. She had helped her younger sister to take care of Marianne as a newborn and felt her loss acutely. Any child's death was a tragedy, of course, but the particular circumstances of Marianne's death, the truth behind the euphemistic letter from the sisters, Anna did not need to be told. Marianne, a sweet, trusting, innocent little girl, had been deemed by the Nazis to be defective, a useless embarrassment. She fell short of the Aryan ideal, and into a perilous category. Hers was a life unworthy of life. They had killed her.

Chapter 47

Ennigerloh, April 1945

Eleanor was now six years old and confident enough with Anna's encouragement, to join the village children in their games.

'Don't wander too far, Eleanor, and stay with the other children.'

'I will, Grandma.'

Some of the girls had dolls, a couple even had prams for them, but they happily shared their scant resources among the group. Eleanor contributed her own doll and took along Herman's wooden cat, allowing it to join in and sleep at the foot of one of the prams. She made sure to bring it back to the safety of her room afterwards, where it lay on a shelf with her dog-eared, almost spineless Klarchen book.

The boys had their own games. They were still enthusiastically fighting the war with planks of wood as guns, and plenty of shouting. One day, not long after Eleanor had arrived, some of the bigger boys approached the group of girls and their dolls game, and the smaller boys who were playing with a ball.

'Hands up!' they ordered, waving their sham weapons menacingly. 'Line up against that wall, and we will shoot you!'

Eleanor turned to look at them. They reminded her of the mean teenage boy she had encountered on first arriving in the mountains, who had put her on the back of the cow. She took a deep breath and set her jaw as she walked up to the biggest boy. She stood before him, feet apart and arms akimbo, glaring up at him.

'If you're going to shoot me with your plank, then shoot. I am not going to stand against the wall.'

The boy blinked at her speechlessly for a moment.

'All right then, girls don't have to.' He mumbled, turning on the smaller boys, the easier targets. They backed, wide-eyed, away from him, only rescued by the call to eat.

'Lunch is ready, children!' and the confrontation was over.

A few days later, the whole gang of children ventured to the edge of the rural village. It was the first warm day of spring and they were in high spirits and played with noisy exuberance.

'You kids!' there was an angry shout that stopped them all in their tracks. They turned as one to see a red-faced farmer appear at the door of the farmhouse. He thundered toward them roaring 'Can't a man have a moment's peace? In the barn with you! Go on, the lot of you, in you go.'

He marched the dozen or so children across the farmyard and into a rickety wooden barn, slamming the door and lowering the wooden latch to trap them inside. The children began to whisper.

'That was Rudy's dad.'

'He was really cross with us.'

'I hope he doesn't tell my mum, I'll be for it.'

'How long do you think he'll leave us for, Rudy?'

Rudy was the big boy who a few days before had threatened Eleanor with a loaded plank. He swaggered around the barn and threw himself on a bale of straw, plucking a stalk to chew and shrugging dismissively.

'Not long. He shouts a lot but he doesn't do anything. I'm not scared of him.'

He closed his eyes and pretended to sleep. The barn was a novel place to play for a while, it smelt of sweet straw and warm animals and was full of interesting farm tools.

'What was that?' said a girl, in alarm.

'What?' Rudy opened a disinterested eye.

'That! Didn't you hear it? A scratching sound, there's something there, behind the water trough.'

Rudy sat up, grinning with mischief.

'A rat, most likely.'

Predictably, the girl screamed, triggering a chain reaction among the younger children.

'I'm scared.'

'I want to go home.'

"I want my mum,' with tearful eyes the children looked to Rudy as the oldest, and the heir apparent of the barn, to save them.

'Look here! I think we can squeeze through this gap,' called Eleanor from the back of the barn. She had spotted a hole in the wall where the planks were loose. It would not take much effort to pull a couple of them away so at least the smaller children would be able to escape without the farmer knowing. It would serve him right, thought Eleanor, to believe he had lost a whole village's children for a while.

'No!' said Rudy sharply, 'No. We can't do that.'

'Why not?' said Eleanor. Surely he did not like being locked in here any more than the rest of them?

'We just can't, that's all. He'll have to let us out eventually, all your parents will be wondering where you are.'

Rudy was red faced, his eyes darted left and right anxiously. You are scared of him, thought Eleanor. You are nothing but a bully. You pick on the smaller children, but when your dad is angry, you're just as scared as they are. She sat on a bale with her back to Rudy and her arms crossed, annoyed at his cowardice until his mother came to free them.

Eleanor liked playing with the other children. On one of their expeditions they came across another barn at the other end of the village, smaller than the one they had been locked up in, and open at the end. An old man sat on a rustic wooden stool next to a heavy work bench, concentrating intently on his task. The other children moved on past the barn to a patch of grass for a ball game, but Eleanor stayed at the doorway, watching him. He was stitching something out of thick leather, she could not make out what, but she was fascinated by his process. Grandma sewed things all the time, but not like this. Punch a hole, feed a needle through, feed another back the other way, pull the threads tight, punch another hole. She breathed the comforting, warm honey tobacco scent of the leather and looked on, entranced. Feed a needle through, feed another back the other way.

'Hello,' she said nervously, when he eventually felt her eyes on him and looked up. He nodded in acknowledgment.

'Do you want to see?' he said. His voice was gruff, but not unkind, and his skin, even before the spring sun had properly warmed, was brown as the leather he was working and deeply lined around his eyes. Crow's feet, Grandma called it. The stubble on his chin was as white as the close-cropped hair on his head, and he had the bluest eyes Eleanor had ever seen. But it was his hands that entranced her. They were strong and calloused, workman's hands, but deft too, animating his tools with skillful efficiency. Eleanor nodded and stepped forward.

'My grandma taught me sewing, but she doesn't do it like this.'

'You have to punch a hole first, it's too thick, see, to just push a needle through. Then you have to push a second one the other way through the same hole, that makes a stitch on both sides, see, then pull it tight, tight as you can, to make a good firm seam.'

Eleanor smiled at the man. She looked around the barn and could see all manner of things hanging across the back wall. Beautiful, gleaming, useful things, bags and satchels, cases and clogs, he must have stitched them all like this. The tools of his trade were neatly stored on a rack, knives and cutters, dowels, chisels, the handles all worn smooth and oiled from years, perhaps decades, productively spent in his hands.

'Is your Grandma good with a needle, then?' he asked.

'Yes, she's very good, she makes everything,' said Eleanor proudly, holding the sides of her skirt out to illustrate. He cast a brief appraising glance and nodded again, one artisan appreciating the skill of another, before returning to his work. Eleanor understood there was no need to say anything more, she leaned against the wall of the barn and watched the rhythmic punch, stitch, stitch, pull progress of the seam for a while longer, then she ran home to tell Grandma about it.

Back at the Hermeier's house, Anna too had news.
'We're going to move into the hotel, Eleanor, the one opposite the church.'
'Oh,' said Eleanor, deflated. 'Don't Mr and Mrs Hermeier want us here anymore?'
'It's not that, it's just that they need the space for some other visitors. Inge, and her mother, and her three sisters are coming to stay.'
Anna smiled at Eleanor's delighted face, she was thrilled at the thought of seeing her cousin again, and meeting her sisters too.

Chapter 48

Aunt Agnes and her four remaining daughters arrived in Ennigerloh just ahead of the American army. After six long years, the war was finally ending. When Eleanor and Inge wandered the streets around the Hermeier house, there were makeshift white flags hanging from many of the windows in surrender. Pillowcases, tea towels, white cloths of any description were used, whatever the household could find, and the girls giggled at the white flag of last resort, a pair of long-legged bloomers.

They soon grew used to the sight of foreign soldiers in the village. The children thought the soldiers seemed friendly, and Eleanor wished she could remember the English words Mummy had taught her, but that was such a very long time ago.

One day, when Eleanor had been playing with Inge and was walking back to the hotel on her own, she heard a low, soft voice calling.

'Hey, little girl!' she looked around and saw a group of soldiers standing across the road, one of them beckoning her over. She was not sure what to do and took a few tentative steps toward them before stopping still.

The soldier walked away from his friends toward her.

'Don't worry, I'm not gonna hurt you. You like chocolate, don't you? Here, take it, you can have it.'

He held out a large bar of chocolate, but Eleanor could only stare up at him, transfixed. She had not understood his words, although she knew what the chocolate bar was, and she could tell from the lazy, mellow lyricism of his voice that the offering was made with kindness. She knew as well, that it was rude to stare, but she could not tear her eyes away from him. Eleanor had never seen anyone with skin as dark as his. The man's eyes were dancing and he smiled a broad smile which she could not help returning.

'Dankeschon,' she said, taking the chocolate, 'thank you.'

'English! You're welcome!' he laughed.

Eleanor was still smiling when she arrived back at the hotel, where she found Grandma sitting at a table with the hotel owner and a few other women, playing cards. With innate good manners, she broke her bar of chocolate into pieces on a plate and passed it around the table. When the plate returned to Eleanor, it was bare.

'Oh dear,' said Anna, 'there's none left!'

'I expect she's already had her piece,' said one of the women. But Eleanor had not. Next time, she thought, I'll be just a little bit less polite.

The following day, Eleanor walked back to the street where she had met the soldier. She saw a group of them, standing where they had been yesterday and stopped at a distance, looking to see if he was among them. One of the soldiers saw her, and nudged the man next to him, who turned around. It was him! He walked across the road toward her.

'Hey! Little girl, back again?' His eyes were still dancing to the easy rhythm of his voice and Eleanor smiled shyly at him, gazing at his uncommon skin. He crouched down to talk to her.

'You come for more chocolate? Sorry, I don't have any more to give you.'

Still she gazed at him. He laughed, shaking his head.

'Alright, run along now,' he sauntered back to his friends, leaving her empty handed. But Eleanor was satisfied. She had not returned for more chocolate, she had just wanted another look at the man with the beautiful, extraordinary dark skin.

Chapter 49

Some weeks later, it was finally arranged that Wilhelm would be able to collect Anna and Eleanor from Ennigerloh and take them home to Neuss. By now, the British Army were in control of the region and with the war so recently ended, travel was still very difficult. Even if permits and a reliable vehicle could be obtained, the road and rail infrastructure was demolished to the point that it was almost unnavigable. Their journey was only possible as a detour of a business trip, and Wilhelm appeared in Ennigerloh behind the wheel of his flatbed truck, with an additional trailer attached, both of which had seen better days. The truck and trailer were both filled with pieces of the copper machinery of Wilhelm's business.   Only one useable seat remained in the cab, so a bale of straw was squeezed in behind the cab in the open back of the lorry, as a makeshift bench.

Anna and Eleanor watched the sun rise as they left Ennigerloh, huddled together on the straw bale, leaning against the back of the cab. It was a slow, jolting journey west. Besides navigating the road blocks and bomb craters, more than once the truck broke down and necessitated some dogged searching by Wilhelm to find a garage with any kind of tools that could get it running again. Eventually, nearing the curfew time, soldiers at a checkpoint directed them to a place where they could stop for the night. It was spring and the temperature dropped quickly once the sun went down. All Anna had to cover them with were a couple of black crepe scarves and an umbrella. They formed a tent with the sheer fabric over their heads, and spent a surprisingly warm, dry night on their straw bale in the back of the truck.

At sunrise they shook the dew from their makeshift shelter and began another day as tedious as the last.

After hours of slow, intermittent progress, Anna said

'Look, Eleanor, we are not far away now, this town is called Essen.'

Eleanor looked all around, but she could not see a town, only an eerie wasteland of rubble under a thick blanket of dust. The truck and trailer rattled on.

Late in the afternoon, they reached Dusseldorf, and made their way south, following the bank of the wide Rhine river. They could see Neuss on the opposite bank, but the road bridges were all bombed, there was no way to get across. They trundled on, and came across a temporary pontoon, made of a line of small boats roped together, with planks of wood laid across the top. It was a fragile structure, built for the lightest of traffic, certainly not for an unreliable, fully laden lorry and trailer, but it was the only route across the river.

Wilhelm eased the truck slowly down the steep bank and with great concentration lined up the wheels with the pontoon planks. They inched cautiously across, Eleanor hiding under Anna's black scarf, too scared to look. The pontoon swayed with the flow of the river, but Wilhelm held his nerve, held the truck's line, and whistled with relief as the front wheels got a purchase on the opposite bank. He powered the engine to get the rest of the rig off the pontoon and drive up the slope, but this was too much for the truck, and once more, it cut out. They started to slip backwards, down the bank toward the river. Anna and Eleanor clung desperately to each other as they slid, out of control. The back wheels were about to plunge into the river when suddenly the trailer twisted sideways. The truck's tailgate slammed into the skewed front of the trailer with a crash, and the whole vehicle stopped abruptly, awkwardly jammed together at the water's edge.

They had narrowly escaped total disaster, but still they were stuck at the foot of a steep bank, in a twisted, spent vehicle, weighed down with machinery. It was several hours before the truck could be persuaded up the bank, and by now, they were late for the curfew.

Wilhelm rolled the truck slowly along the familiar side streets of Neuss, killing the engine and the headlights when a patrol jeep neared. They crept the short distance from the river to Kanalstrasse, avoiding detection until they were within sight of their building, when an unseen British army jeep pulled across their path and stopped in front of them. The patrol alighted and walked toward them. Wilhelm helped Anna down from the truck and lifted Eleanor to stand between them.

'Stay where you are,' came the order form the officer, swiftly translated by his subordinate.

'We are just trying to get home,' explained Wilhelm.

'It is after the curfew. Travel is not permitted at this time,' said the officer.

Anna stepped forward, drawing herself up to her full diminutive height, the rolled umbrella in her hand. All her life, and especially throughout the war years, she had put her family's interests above all else, and she was not about to stop now.

'My good man, believe me, we do not want to be travelling now. We have been travelling for two long days in this crate, and our home is there, right behind you,' she pointed the furled umbrella at the upstairs windows of their building. 'You are British,' she continued, transferring the umbrella's aim to the officer, 'this child, too, is British,' she placed her free hand on Eleanor's shoulder. Eleanor dared not move. She hardly dared breathe.

'And tonight, this British child will sleep in her bed, in her home, in that building.' Again, the umbrella indicated her target. 'Tomorrow, I will speak to your commanding officer, but tonight, we are going home.'

The translator relayed her speech to the officer, who raised his eyebrows but decided on the diplomatic route. He cleared his throat and gave orders that nothing be taken from the truck until tomorrow, when his commanding officer would be informed of their misdemeanour. They would, of course, be required to register their presence in any case. The family were duly escorted to their door. That night Eleanor slept in her mother's old bed, tucked in under the green satin eiderdown in the attic room beneath the eaves.

Chapter 50

Cairo, April 1945

The German diplomatic legation finally set sail on 19 April 1945, on the Swedish ship the SS Drottningholm, bound for Hamburg out of Istanbul. Hildegard was not there to witness their departure, she was embarking on a journey of her own.

An unexpected package had been delivered to her, via the British Consulate, containing her salvation in the form of a rail ticket for the Taurus Express, travel permits and two pairs of trapezium shaped, felt epaulette badges, one green, one black, each identifying her in gold embroidery as a British War Correspondent and legitimising her passage through the chaos. Finally, miraculously, there was confirmation of her ongoing travel to England.

She marvelled at every item as it came out of the envelope, at a loss to understand where it had all come from.

Sir. It could only have been him. Who else knew Hildegard's truth?

Who else would have had enough influence to arrange these things for her? Who else knew about the risks she had taken in the name of the Allied cause? The many German documents she had read upside down across a consular desk and later, in the little back parlour, recalled and translated with photographic accuracy. The many more papers she had stolen when the opportunity arose, and delivered with haste, aware of the time imperative. Who else had known of the discomfort that dealing with a man like Wolff had caused her, a Gestapo in the same repellent form as so many others she had encountered, his rabid Nazism only curtailed by his exile in a foreign land? She had suffered too, first the nationalistic extreme of Scarlat Urlateanu's beliefs that tipped over the brink into fascism, and his passionate tirade on the distorted, ugly utopia that was the beloved Rumania of his imagination. Then, the blade against her throat, his very real threat to her life.

She had faced cold, ruthless Ludwig, whose insidious influence would not leave Istanbul with him, but would remain in the agents he had left here waiting, ready to rise up in the name of fascism.

Finally, the quietest, most painful injustice, her necessary rejection by the British community. Hildegard had always understood that she must appear loyal to Germany in Istanbul, she must not arouse suspicion or she would be of no use in her task. It had worked, the Nazis she had encountered had trusted her, considered her straightforward, but it had hurt her that William Burland, and others, had spoken so disparagingly about her. They did not know her truth, they did not know her real allegiance nor the strength of her commitment. They could not know, if they had known, her work could have been compromised. She knew that she would never be able to explain herself to any of them, never tell them what she had done, what she had risked in their shared interest.

But Sir knew. He had not forgotten her, nor had he abandoned her and that was vindication that she had done something good, something useful.

As the SS Drottningholm cast off from Istanbul, Hildegard boarded the Taurus Express, bound for Cairo. The rhythmic, clicking sway of the train was soporific, but Hildegard was too excited to sleep. She looked out at the changing colours of the Levant, the lush green citrus groves, the dry ochre desert, the distant purple mountains to the left, and the sparkling blue sea to the right.

On the rare sorties of the guard through the carriage, she pulled her coat over the stowaway Mr Mouse, who lay still and quiet until the guard had gone, complicit in this final deception. The relentless travel was lightened a little by the pleasant company of a Captain Wateridge, who joined the train at Aleppo, but Hildegard was relieved, nonetheless, when they eventually drew to a halt at Cairo station. She waited on the platform as the porter stacked her luggage and the train wheezed out its final exhausted exhalation of steam around her.

'H! Hildegard!' a grinning Sam ran toward her, and wrapped his arms around her, until Mr Mouse nosed himself between them, keen to be included. Sam loosened his hold enough to look at her.

'You look well, Hildegard, you had a good trip?'

'Not too bad. I'm just so very glad to be here.' She smiled at him, tired from travelling but happier than she had been for months.

'What about you, Mouse, you reprobate? You're filthy, what happened to you?' Sam had knelt to rub the dog's ears but stopped when he saw that one was torn, and there was a deep scratch under Mr Mouse's eye.

'Hmm, there was small altercation with another canine in Maltepe, wasn't there Mouse? We'll say no more about it,' said Hildegard with mock terseness.

'I bet the other guy came off worse, right, Mouse?' Mr Mouse wagged his tail, happy to be reunited with his friend.

'How long before you move on?' Sam asked as they wove their way arm in arm through the crowded station.

'I'm not sure, exactly. There is passage on a ship for me, but no confirmed date. Two or three weeks, I think.'

'Time enough to show you Cairo, then,' grinned Sam, with his usual enthusiasm.

A few days later, Hildegard's quiet morning coffee was interrupted by the repetitious blaring of a car horn underneath her hotel window. She opened the window and leaned out to see what the noise was about. There below was Sam, at the wheel of a borrowed jeep, with a couple of men she did not know in the back. All three were laughing like children and looking up at her expectantly.

'Come on, Hildegard, day trip!' called Sam, over the general din of the bustling street.

'Where to?' she called back, already knowing that it did not matter, she would be going with them.

'Pyramids, of course! Where else?' he said, 'Bring Mouse, come on, let's go.'

Ten minutes later they burst at breakneck speed out of the narrow city streets toward the desert. Suddenly, there was a gunshot loud crack, and Hildegard spun around in alarm.

'Don't worry, just one of these!' The younger of Sam's friends, also called Sam, held up a small torpedo shaped object, then hurled it from the car. It too landed with a loud crack and young Sam whooped, before delving into the sack at his feet for another of the missiles.

They found a local guide outside one of the pyramids, who was willing, for a few coins, to show them its pillaged interior. The magnesium strips that served as torches lit the way with a ghostly white light, and they could barely make out the ancient images on the walls behind their own flickering shadows. They stifled giggles rising in part at young Sam irreverently pretending to be a mummy when the guide was not looking, and in part to hide their nerves at the eeriness of the place.

Bursting back into the bright sunshine at the end of the tour, their joyous VE spirits were instantly restored. It was a raucous day, they laughed a lot and drank more, feeling profoundly happy and grateful to be alive, including Mr Mouse who stood proud between the jeep's seats, taking great gulps of air as they sped along.

Back in their hotel room that evening, Mr Mouse collapsed into instant slumber on the rug, and Hildegard lay in the bath, oddly feeling what Sam would have called a bit blue. Her head was spinning with the overwhelming knowledge that the war in Europe had at last ended, and she was on her way to a new life in England. It was the stuff of dreams, Peter would have said. And yet, so many unknowns worried her, primary among them the fate of her daughter. Was Eleanor still alive? Where was she, and how would she find her?

For herself, Hildegard wondered what kind of reception would greet her in England. She knew she would have to explain herself to the authorities. Even if she were believed, and she could hardly believe everything that had happened herself, would she be welcome? She had done her best, but had it been enough? She hoped to continue working for the nation, to help rebuild it in the new era of peace, but what could she do now to usefully contribute? Where to start with any of it? Come on, Hildegard, she told herself, worrying won't help, you have coped with so much already, you can face whatever lies ahead. The water was almost cold when she stepped out of it and reached for her towel. She pulled the plug and sat on the edge of the tub, watching the sandy silt residue of the day run out with the bathwater.

Chapter 51

Mr Mouse followed Hildegard to the door and lay down on the cool marble floor as she closed it behind her. He would wait by the door, as he always did, until she returned. Hildegard had not found a way to make the relentless Cairo sun weigh lighter on her, despite the most gossamer of summer dresses, but venture into it she must. A wall of midday heat hit her as she stepped out into the street, and she smiled at the thought that here was solid proof that she was an Englishwoman, just as Mr Mouse was very much not a mad dog.

Sam had invited her to lunch at a smart restaurant and when she arrived, she saw him deep in earnest conversation with a man in the uniform of a senior ranking French officer.

'Hildegard,' called Sam, raising his hand to get her attention. As she approached their table the other man stood and held out his hand.

'Madam,' he said, bowing slightly as they shook hands, 'France thanks you. Alas, we cannot give you our Victory Medal, as we are so far from France. Please, accept my own 'baton', pour une femme très brave.'

Hildegard stood speechless as the officer held her hand in both of his for a moment, then nodded at Sam before turning and walking smartly away.

'Well! Who was he, and what was that about?' Hildegard was astonished. She turned the little baton pin over in her palm.

'A friend,' said Sam enigmatically. 'An admirer of your work, I guess.'

He grinned at her. Before she could question him further, he went on

'I think I've found a solution to your problem. But first, what would you like to eat?'

After lunch they returned to Hildegard's hotel, where she handed Sam a neat stack of bank notes.

'Here, the money I owe you. Thank you for the loan.'

Sam had lent Hildegard eleven hundred Turkish lira before he left for Bucharest the previous summer. He was concerned that she should not run out of money, as she had given up her job at Taksim's in order to go into hiding to protect herself from the German repatriations.

During her time in Istanbul, Hildgard had in fact had several sources of income. She had wages from Taksim's, of course, which she supplemented by teaching English to Turkish people in her apartment, the work which William Burland had misinterpreted as a far more ancient and base profession. Then Sir had paid her forty British pounds a month, which she was proud to have earned. Finally, and most difficult for Hildegard, Wolff had also paid her a monthly salary of five hundred Turkish lira.

The money from Wolff had caused Hildegard a degree of turmoil at the start. She found it repellent to be taking Gestapo money, and it further offended her morals to be paid for work that she was actively undermining. But it was part of the role she played, it would have been impossible to refuse payment from Wolff when she needed him to believe she was working honestly for him. Eventually, she persuaded herself to view his money as reparation, compensation from the Gestapo for the pain they had caused her over the years.

'What's that?' said Sam, as Hildegard placed a chamois pouch on the table with a thud.

'Gold sovereigns,' said Hildegard. 'I don't know what to do with them.'

'Where did they come from?' Sam opened the crudely stitched pouch carefully as some of the coins tumbled out. Hildegard would never be as skillful with a needle as her mother.

'I bought them, in the Bazar. All the time in Istanbul, Wolff was paying me. I didn't want to take his money, but there wasn't really any choice, so I thought it best to save it. But now, I don't know what is going to happen to me when I get to England, so I don't know if I should take it with me. But what else can I do with it?'

Sam thought for a minute.

'Leave it with me. I have a friend in the British Embassy here I can give it to for you, for safe keeping. Then there's a chance you will get it back some time.'

'Honestly Sam, I don't care if I don't. I'll be quite happy if I can work for my living when I get to England.'

'I know, but it never hurt to have a nest egg, and anyway, this money is due to you, after everything they put you through.'

'Thank you,' Hildegard sighed, relieved to have a solution.

'What for?' Sam laughed, then stopped as he saw her blink the dampness away from her eyes. She squeezed his hand.

'For everything. For helping me, for having a plan, for understanding. Thank you, Sam.'

Chapter 52

The day before Hildegard was to leave Cairo she began her sad farewells. The problem to which Sam had told her in the restaurant that he had found a solution, was what to do with Mr Mouse. With shipping so overstretched, and such vast numbers of people to repatriate, a dog was not permitted to take up space aboard ship. Mr Mouse would have to stay in Cairo.

Sam had managed to find him a home and had thoughtfully arranged for Hildegard to visit in advance to allay her fears for Mouse's future. The Garzouzi's were a warm and welcoming family who lived in a beautiful house and Hildegard felt reassured that Mr Mouse would be loved, but it was hard to leave him all the same. The family discreetly left them alone in the kitchen for their final goodbye.

Hildegard felt slightly ridiculous explaining to Mr Mouse that she must go, and she could not take him with her, but she felt she owed him that, even if he was just a dog. He had been her daily companion for a year and a half, during which there had been times when she had had nobody except for Mr Mouse. He sat tall and straight on the terracotta tiles, listening with an air of quiet dignity.

Eventually she forced herself to leave and for the first time in his life Mr Mouse did not follow Hildegard to the door.

The following morning, she said goodbye to Sam, too. They parted early at her hotel, with her luggage stacked around them ready to be collected for the train to Alexandria.

'I know you've had a rough time,' he told her, 'but going back to England now is what you hoped for, it's what you want, isn't it?'

She nodded, trying to force a brave smile onto her miserable, tear stained face. Through all the trials of the last two years, he had been her friend, her guardian, her love and she would miss him.

'It is what I want, Sam, more than anything. It's what I have dreamed of, but I'm afraid too, I don't know what the future holds for me in England. I don't know if I will find Eleanor again, I'm not even sure she is still alive. And I know I'm very lucky to be going, but still it's frightening.'

The ship sailed from Alexandria that afternoon with most of the passengers gathered aft and port side, calling and waving to those on the quay who had come to wish them bon voyage. There was nobody on the dock waving to Hildegard but she did not mind. She preferred not to dwell on all that she was leaving behind. Instead, she made her way along the quieter starboard deck to the bow, where she leaned on the railing and looked forward to England.

Afterword

The SS Drottningholm sailed from Istanbul on 19 April 1945. During the voyage, Wolff had reconsidered Ferruh's suggestion that he apply for asylum. He had attempted to do so when they called at Lisbon, in the hope of securing an assurance from Turkey before they reached Sweden. No assurance was received, and while they were at sea on the next leg of their journey, Germany capitulated.

The SS Drottningholm docked at Liverpool on 26 May 1945. Wolff and Ludwig were among the German officials arrested on board and transferred to London for interrogation.

Scarlat Urlateanu eventually returned to Rumania. In 1951 he was among thousands sentenced by the Communist regime to internal exile on the Baragan Steppe, in a dark reflection of the pastoral idyll that he had imagined for the peasant classes in his dream of a Rumanian utopia many years before. The Domicil Obligaturs, those under house arrest, were abandoned without shelter, food, water or medicines, and left to fend for themselves on this bleak unforgiving plain in south east Rumania.

Most of the deportees were released in 1955, after Rumania failed to gain membership of the United Nations on the grounds of human rights abuses.

Political prisoners were detained until a general pardon was issued in 1964. The charges against Scarlat Urlateanu were suspicion of anti-Communist activities and membership of the Iron Guard.

Sam Pope Brewer continued to work for the New York Times for many years, reporting from all over the world. He married in 1949 and had one child. The marriage ended in the late 1950's while they were living in Beirut, when his wife left him for his friend Kim Philby, whom she later followed to Russia.

Sir remained in his secret world, apart from a brief foray into the limelight, also concerning Kim Philby, whereby many years after she had known him, Hildegard finally discovered his name. He was Nicholas Elliott.

Peter, Hildegard's Hungarian friend, was Peter Sugar, who achieved his dream of living in America where he went on to become Professor Emeritus of Eastern European History at Washington University. They remained lifelong friends.

Hildegard came to England and as she had anticipated, was obliged to explain herself to the British authorities. Once her story had been verified and accepted, she set about doing what she could to help straighten the post-war chaos.

She traced Bern through his bank, and they arranged to meet on a small country railway station in Gloucestershire. Following that encounter, they did not resume their relationship.

In 1947 she was at last able to bring Eleanor, by then almost nine years old, to England. In the meantime, the clumsily sewn chamois pouch that she had left with Sam in Cairo had inexplicably appeared on her work desk one day. The gold sovereigns were still inside, and she used them then to fund her training as a physiotherapist, a career that she loved. Reparation.

In 1961, not long after Eleanor was married, Hildegard accepted a job in Canada and flew out to begin a new life. Within a couple of days, she had a catastrophic fall on some ice and lay for several hours before anyone found her. Her hip was badly broken and although it healed, she always needed a stick to walk with from then on.

Epilogue

England, November 1965

Kasper Champion inspects himself in the bathroom mirror. He rubs his hand along his clean shaven jaw, checks his freshly barbered short back and sides is neatly combed, he is satisfied that he looks respectable. He puts on the jacket to his slim cut suit and makes a final adjustment to the tie already perfectly knotted over his collar button. It is Saturday, and he is not going to work today, but it is important that he looks smart. Today he has a mission.

It is a self-appointed mission, granted. He is still too junior to be sent into the field for the Service officially, but he considers it the right thing to do nonetheless. He takes his raincoat from the hook as he leaves and closes the door carefully behind him. As he walks down the stairs, he sees his landlady returning to the kitchen with the post.

'You're out early on a Saturday,' she stops to talk to him.

'Yes. I've a few things to do today. See you later, Mrs Jones,' he is polite but continues purposefully for the front door. He has neither the time nor the inclination for one of her chats this morning.

He reaches the platform five minutes before the train, just as planned. It is gratifyingly on time, and he finds a seat and settles down to look out of the window. He is thinking about the day ahead.

Kasper is proud to work for the Service. Proud to have signed the Official Secrets Act and undertaken to do whatever is necessary to protect the country's security. It was relatively early days for him, so to date that had involved mostly the moving around of files from one office to another, in and out of the archive, that sort of thing. It was quite dull, if he was honest. At least, it had been until last week.

Last week, he had been given a stack of manilla folders and a new task. He was to read through the files and set aside those that contained references to certain people, one of whom was an officer of the Service who had risen through the ranks to the highest level. Kasper had caught a glimpse of him once or twice, a tall, slender man, energetic and animated, even in middle-age. Everybody in the building knew who he was, his reputation within the Service was legendary. There had been only one misstep, as far as Kasper was aware. That had generated a brief flurry of media attention a few years previously, around the same time that Kasper was approached at Cambridge and invited to come to London after graduation. His curiosity piqued by the story in the news, he had accepted. Now here he was, studying files detailing the most secret life's work of this unknown national hero. Kasper could quite see why references to any part of an almost impeccable career should remain secret. Who knew what connections might be made if any of it were to become public? He completely understood why the history of this great servant of the service should be redacted and concealed.

Kasper had conscientiously trawled the files he was allocated. His pile documented the interrogation reports of aliens arriving in England around the end of the Second World War, twenty years before. They were mostly a bunch of irrelevant ne'erdowells, some genuine refugees, and a few who had actually contributed to the Allied war effort. But there was one file that had stood out for him. It was the number of the file that first caught his attention. Kasper had always been drawn to patterns of numbers. He looked for them, for the links between numbers, without even thinking about it. The numbers on the files he had been given all followed the same format, two letters then a series of numbers and within that, he noticed, there were different sequences. A group of people who had been arrested together might have a consecutive set of numbers allocated to their files, for example. Or people who had originated from the same country might share the same prefix of numbers. The number on this particular file though, was unique. Other than the standard format, it bore no resemblance to any other file number.

The file contained the notes of an interrogation from the Women's Reception Centre, in London, in the summer of 1945. A German woman, British by marriage, who claimed to have been an agent for the Service luminary in question, in Istanbul. She had not known who the man was, of course, and he had moved on by the time of her interrogation in any case, so it had taken some time to verify her story.

Kasper read the file from cover to cover, impressed by the risks she had taken to help the Allies. At least, that was what she had claimed. The interrogating officer had clearly been sceptical, he had heard it all before, or versions of it, and was reserving judgment until a response was received.

The senior officer of the Service, Sir, had responded. He had read the interrogation report, looked at the photographs and confirmed that Mrs Reilly had indeed been his agent in Istanbul. She was, he said, probably the best female agent in the city. Which was high praise, Kasper thought, given which city it was and when she had lived there.

Mrs Reilly had been allowed to remain in England, with her British nationality confirmed. Whatever her feelings had been about this, it was not enough for Kasper. He knew that this woman's achievements would never come to light, he himself was under orders to bury them. He doubted that this would trouble her at all. If she were the sort to seek publicity, he reasoned, she would have done so by now. The Service would have denied it all, of course, but there had been no need, in the intervening years she had vanished into anonymity.

Kasper was aware from the file that there had been others in that time and place, who did not know Mrs Reilly's true purpose and might, in their ignorance, be unkind and indiscreet in talking about her. There would be oblique references to her in other files that might eventually surface into the public domain. Untruths and partial truths that were not Hildegard Reilly's truth. There was not much he could about that, unfair though it was. But this he could do. This one thing, his mission for today.

He leaves the station and finds a café for tea and toast, there was no time for breakfast before he left. Afterwards, he walks back along the main street, toward the turning for her address. It was straightforward to find in the telephone directory. She has an unusual first name and she is not too far out of London. She has a private physiotherapy practise now, apparently. Good for her.

A woman comes out of a shop just in front of him. Kasper stands still and watches her intently. She thanks the shopkeeper as she closes the door behind her. She is carrying a parcel which she tucks under her arm carefully, she looks pleased with her purchase. She starts to walk away from the shop, leaning on the walking stick in her other hand, and Kasper notices that the sole of one of her shoes is built up. This is not a temporary injury, then. He reaches the shop and sees that it sells things for babies. A quick deduction tells him that her daughter would be in her twenties by now, perhaps there is a grandchild? A baby girl, judging by the pink ribbon on the parcel she was carrying.
It is her, he is sure of it. He knows her from the photographs in her file. They are twenty years old but she has hardly changed at all. It is definitely her. Have a care Kasper, he warns himself. Remember you know her, she does not know you.

Hildegard pulls her coat closer around her neck as she continues toward her home, walking deliberately, lopsidedly with her stick. Kasper crosses the road and walks briskly until he is ahead of her, then crosses back. He wants to approach her face to face, so as not to alarm her. He stops in front of her and clears his throat.

'Mrs Reilly?' he asks. Hildegard studies his face. He is young, but he does not look like some of the young people these days. He has a short, neat haircut and wears a grey suit and tie under a mackintosh that flapped open as he walked toward her. He ties the belt to tidy his appearance. Hildegard does not recognise him.

'I'm sorry, have we met?' Hildegard's voice is low in timbre like tumbling pebbles, from decades of cigarettes. It is steady but guarded.

'You are her, aren't you? Hildegard Reilly? I know what you did,' he blurts out and immediately reproaches himself.

'I don't know what you're talking about,' she says evenly, betraying no emotion. He takes a deep breath. The last thing he wants is to offend her, he must calm down.

'During the war,' he continues earnestly, 'I know what you did, during the war.'

Hildegard sets her jaw and stares levelly at him. He continues talking, he is committed now.

'I just wanted to tell you, well, to thank you, really, for what you did. I think you were very brave.'

There. He has said it. He has acknowledged her. She gazes at him.

There is a silent, impotent storm in her grey eyes. She remembers all of it, every terrifying, exhilarating, heart-breaking, justified moment. She smiles a small, secret smile and almost imperceptibly nods her head. Kasper smiles back, and for a moment they are connected. He turns and watches as with the last, yellowed-lace birch leaves dancing across the path in front of her, she makes her way slowly home.

Author's Note

I have always known what my grandmother was during the war. My schoolfriends' grandmothers were factory workers or land girls, nurses, drivers, any number of useful contributors to the war effort. And mine was a spy.

I knew what she was, but I didn't know what she actually did. It was one of those family legends that is always mentioned but never talked about. It wasn't until my mother became ill and we were spending hours together in the car as I drove her to consultant's appointments and medical treatment that we really started talking about her family. I asked her about her father, Bernard, whose name I knew, but little else, and it turned out that she knew barely more than I did.

Then we talked about her mother, Hildegard, who I remembered well from my childhood. I asked about her legendary wartime activities, but my mother knew precious little about that either. Certainly not any details. She did remember though that she had kept Hildegard's diaries and she would see if she could find them.

Miraculously, thirty years and two house moves since Hildegard died, Eleanor still had the diaries. I found them fascinating. There was poetry, personal reflections, a lot about trees and dogs, and some stories from the war that often raised more questions than they answered.

And there was a newspaper cutting from the New York Times, the obituary of a man called Sam Pope Brewer, who had died in the 1970's. Neither mum nor I knew who he was, but he had clearly meant something to Hildegard, so I started my research with him.

I discovered that Sam was a prolific journalist, whose personal archive was in boxes in a university library in Wisconsin, USA. At the time, it wasn't possible for me to go there, but the library sent me their list of approved researchers who might act on our behalf. Among them, serendipitously, was Gregory Smith of History Piquette, whose particular interest was the secret intelligence world during the war, and who was available to take on the research immediately.

Within weeks of our first contact, Greg had spent days in the library diligently searching through and photographing Sam's lifetime body of work and personal papers for any mention of Hildegard.

He struck gold with Sam's diaries for the war years and sent us hundreds of images of documents which told us much more of the story of Sam and Hildegard in Istanbul and Cairo. The picture was becoming clearer.

My next port of call was the National Archives in Kew. I had the names of some of the Germans from Istanbul and discovered that their interrogation files were in the public domain. I spent days wading through stacks of the old manilla files, wondering who among them had known my grandmother and what secrets the frequent yellow redaction slips were keeping. Finally, among the pages of the hefty files for Bruno Wolff and Thomas Ludwig, there again was Hildegard.

And there too, pencilled in the margin of one of Wolff's papers, was a Personal File number for Reilly. This would be the transcript of her interrogation on arriving in England in 1945. But there was no file, and no other mention of one. The government department that holds and releases these records would neither confirm nor deny the existence of Hildegard's file.

It took some time to accept that I now knew as much as I ever would about my grandmother. It occurred to me that, whilst I may never read the official version she gave to the authorities on arriving in England, the fact that she was allowed to remain freely in the UK surely indicates that her story was verified and she was accepted as friend not foe. Whatever details might be missing, it is enough to know that she was strong, and brave, and resilient and she did her best to do the right thing. I am proud of her.

Hildegard is mentioned in a couple of published works already. She is the German woman who works at Taksim's and tries to get British and American customers talking. She is in contact with the Germans, she works for them, she has a dubious reputation.

Having read the original documents publicly available I can see these authors' sources of information. Sir's reports to Security and Intelligence Middle East (SIME) Headquarters in Cairo, where he deliberately reinforced the impression that she was in league with the Nazi's in order to bury her secret alliance with him. Correspondence from William (Bill) Harris Burland praising Sam, but denouncing Hildegard. The interrogation transcripts for the Germans captured on the SS Drottningholm who considered her genuine in her allegiance to them, testament to her success in her task of convincing them of that. Most of these sources did not know the whole story, except for Sir, whose job it was to keep secrets. As a result, research based solely on the information in the public domain is inherently skewed.

Hildegard's diary notes provided her own story, and Sam his. Both added new dimensions to the existing public record. The reason for this book is to give Hildegard a voice, to tell her own war story in its entirety. I hope I have done her justice.

This has been a long project, and over the years I have had such support from many people that I would like to acknowledge.

First, Steve, you make all things possible. Thank you. And thanks to Sean and Kieran, just for being you.

Thanks to Tess and Chris, for encouraging the story to be told. It is yours too.

Thanks to Pat and Malc, for your quiet, constant support through all this time, it has not gone unnoticed and it means a lot.

Thanks to my good friends Helen, Paula and Anita, for early proof-reads of the book and your endless patience while I talk about it. Endlessly.
Thanks especially to Helen, for accompanying me on my pilgrimage to Berlin and making that so much more fun than it otherwise would have been. We experienced more serendipity in the process as we arrived at the Humboldt University building at the same moment as a young man on a bicycle. He turned out to be the architect responsible for the recent refurbishment of the building, who explained how he had wanted to preserve the story of the place. He showed us the holes in the outside wall from Russian bullets fired in the street fighting at the fall of Berlin. And we went inside, right up to the tiny attics inhabited by Anna, Hildegard and Eleanor, so small the architect could not believe anyone could have lived there. They had been bombed out of existence a few weeks after my family left, but are now restored.

Thanks also to the many other friends who took the time to read earlier versions and whose opinions have helped to shape the book.

Thanks to Gregory Smith, of History Piquette, for your enthusiastic, thorough and efficient research, and your continued interest in the project.

Finally, some notes on accuracy. I have tried to make this story as close to Hildegard's truth as possible. Some of the details were dependent on the early childhood memories of woman by then in her seventies, my mother Eleanor. Those facts that could be checked, she had been surprisingly accurate about, so I have some confidence that the rest of what she recalled is equally reliable.

Within all the documents I researched, there were various references to, and spellings of, Romania. In the interests of consistency I have used 'Rumania' throughout. This was the most common contemporary spelling I came across, but there were also 'Roumania' and occasionally 'Romania', as is currently used. I chose the version that was in most frequent use at the time, also I thought it was helpful to distinguish that country from that of the present day, a different place.

In the interests of transparency, I want to acknowledge the few elements that I have invented.

First, some names that I have allocated. Reinhardt, Hildegard's Nazi student at the Berlitz School in Berlin, and all the people who lived in Kiesewald, Maria, Erika and Hedda Braun, Klaus, Erika's boyfriend, and Max the wheelbarrow smuggler. Their stories are as Eleanor recalled, but she could not remember their names. All other names are real.

Second, Kasper Champion is a fictional character. Sometime during the 1960's a man, a stranger, did approach Hildegard in the street and thank her for her wartime service, but she had no idea who he was. There are a very limited number of candidates who could have been privy to this information. I created Kasper to illustrate this story, but also as a means of offering a scenario in which there is a reason for Hildegard's Personal File to be unavailable. There is no record of 'Sir', Nicholas Elliott, in the National Archive either.

Descriptions of the broader events of the war are given in good faith for context, and any errors are entirely my own.

January 2023

Anna and Eleanor

Mouse

Sam

Hildegard and Mr Mouse

Printed in Great Britain
by Amazon